Rainbow Runner by Krista D'Vincent
(See page 35)

Detail of Kimono Jacket
by Carol Marsh Hobday *(See page 8)*

Photographs by Grenier-Ducharme Photography

Joan's Jacket by Joan Siegel
(See page 78)

Photograph by Stuart Golder

Photograph by Stuart Golder

Shawl by Joan Siegel *(See page 80)*

Photograph by Mr. King

Tapestry Bags by Bucky King
(See page 31)

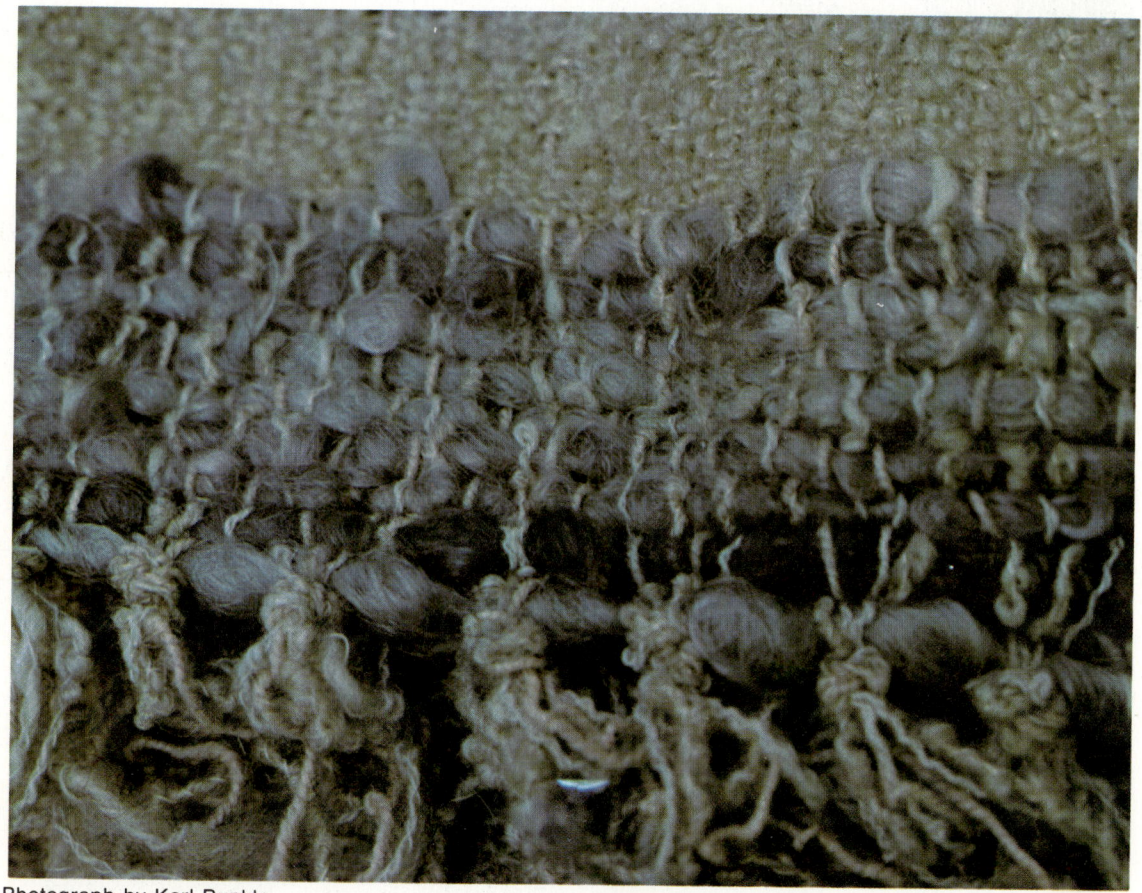

Photograph by Karl Runkle

Detail of Woven Stole by Barbara L. Anderson
(See page 3)

Björknas Harvest by Deborah Daw
(See page 10)

Photograph by David Cluer

Desert Sun by Roz Shirley
(See page 59)

Photograph by Mary Ellen Schultz

The Handspun Project Book

Edited by Deborah Kahn

Select Books

A book almost always reflects the contributions of many people. This book consists entirely of such contributions; it is truly a community effort. I would like to thank: Shuttle, Spindle & Dyepot for publishing the item in Tabby that brought me together with most of the contributors ... Sheila MacEwan and Betty E.M. Jacobs for a generous supply of encouragement and interest ... Rose Perl for being my aunt, teaching me to knit and spin, founding Select Books and being herself ... my mother for much help, patience, encouragement, advice and enthusiasm.

Cover: Joan Siegel modeling her "Mable Poncho" along with George (the Mule), Mable and Mable's lamb. Photograph by Stuart Golder.

Layout & Design — Annette Orban and Midge Kennedy

Diagrams — Carol Marsh Hobday

Yarn Photographs — Barry Kahn

Typesetting — Marilyn McDonald, Aquarian Age Typography

Printing — Cienega Lithographers

All rights reserved. No part of this book may be reproduced without permission in writing from the publisher, except by a reviewer, who may quote brief passages or reproduce illustrations in a review with appropriate credit; nor may any part of this book be reproduced, stored in a retrieval system, or transmitted in any form or by any means — electronic, photocopying, recording, or other — without permission in writing from the publisher.

Copyright © 1978 by Deborah Kahn
Library of Congress Catalog Card Number 78-64613
ISBN 910458-13-8
Select Books
Route 1, Box 129C
Mountain View, Missouri 65548

She seeks wool and flax, and works with willing hands.
Proverbs 31:13

Table of Contents

Barbara L. Anderson — *Equipment Description..........1*
Dog Hair Pillows
Woven Stole
Crocheted Shawl
Weed Bag
"Brown Ripples"

Carol Marsh Hobday — *Kimono Jacket..........8*

Deborah Daw — *"Björknäs Harvest"..........10*

Odessa Vasquez — *White Bedspread..........11*
Striped Bedspread with Handspun Warp
Bag in Bound Weave
Hanging

Faith Tsukroff Wilson
Judy Tsukroff — *Gloves..........18*

Margaret Zeps — *Crocheted Vest..........21*

Joan Z. Rough — *Introduction..........23*
Poncho
Pullover Sweater
Child's Cardigan and Matching Cap
Baby Blanket
Conclusion

Bucky King — *Tapestry Bags..........31*

Janet Hetzler — *Knit Circular Mohair Shawl..........31*

Krista D'Vincent — *Introduction..........35*
Rainbow Runner
Inlay Raw Fleece Hangings
Afghan
Swedish Rosepath Rug
Poncho

Julianne Eaton — *Hooded Jacket..........44*

Nancy Piatkowski — *Crocheted Baskets..........47*
Bags of Handspun Karakul

Jean Lindstrand Bartos
Clarence M. Lindstrand — *Handwoven Coat of Handspun Wool..........51*

Hope Parshall — *Cashmere Scarves..........52*
Tote Bag
Hats

Rose Perl — *Knitted Vest..........58*

iv

Roz Shirley	*"Desert Sun"*	59
	"Crocheted Basket with Eggs"	
Elsie Ewbank	*Three Sweaters*	65
Judi Clark	*Superblanket II*	68
Joan Siegel	*Mable Poncho*	73
	Hat and Mittens	
	Joan's Jacket	
	Shawl	
Suppliers		82
Photographers		83
Bibliography		84
Index		85

Knit Circular Mohair Shawl • JANET HETZLER

Introduction

This book came into being as a result of my own lack of creativity. Having learned how to spin yarn, I was having a hard time making anything out of it. There were two areas in which I was deficient: ideas and technical information. Haunting the library in search of help, I found many lovely and useful books on the textile arts. None of them had any information on using handspun yarns. Ideas were easier to find, but not much use without the basic information on techniques. At this point I had a brainstorm. I thought I knew what sort of book I needed. I publish books. Why not put such a book together myself? It seemed reasonable to assume that if I needed it so would other people.

From that point of delighted inspiration I gradually descended into a morass of hard work. As I began to collect projects, it quickly became clear that most of my thinking about the book was very far from what the reality would be. I had imagined a book with a rather rigid format . . . clothing in one section . . . hangings in another . . . all the information neatly organized and standardized. Fortunately, this degree of tidiness never came to pass. Weavers and spinners seem to be extreme individualists — trying to fit their ideas and work into a standard pattern proved to be impossible. The book evolved instead into a collection of projects described and pictured. Each of the contributors to the book discusses her own work, not only the actual processes but also the development of the design.

Many of the best features of the book evolved as I went along — for example, the photos of the yarn samples, which in combination with the numerous close-up photos of the projects provide information about which yarn to use for your purpose. The book includes yarns handspun of mohair, alpaca, llama wool, cashmere, camel down, angora rabbit hair, various dog hairs, and the wool of many breeds of sheep. Unfortunately, my best efforts failed to turn up any projects that use handspun yarns of silk, cotton or yak hair. (It may be possible to correct this oversight in the future.)

There are weaving diagrams and drafts. Sources of fibers and dyes are mentioned in the margins. Reference books used by the various contributors are summarized in the bibliography (as a publisher I was somewhat chagrined by the brevity of the final list).

This is not the definitive book on using handspun yarns. It is probably more useful and more fun than the definitive work will be (if it ever arrives). Since everything described has been made, none of the material is theory. At the same time, the book still has a quality of adventure and exploration, mostly I suspect because none of the participants feels it necessary to say: "There is only one correct way." Editing this book has solved my original problem of finding uses for my handspun yarns. Perhaps it will be useful for a few other people as well.

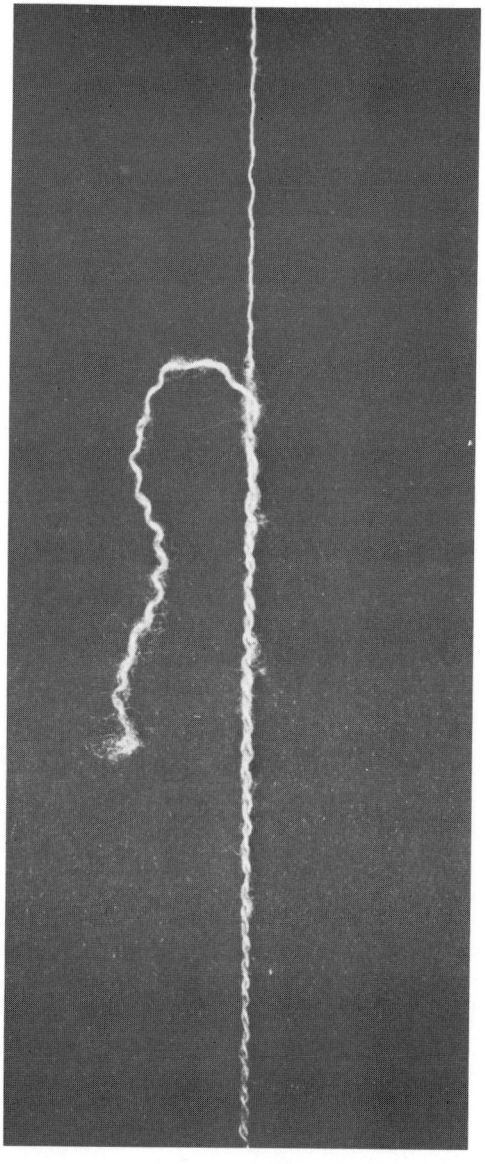

Two ply wool, spun by Elsie Davenport and used for machine knitting by Sheila MacEwan.

Dog hair pillows: light pillow 100% dog hair. Dark pillow black fleece carded with dog hair.

Photograph by Karl Runkle

Photograph by Karl Runkle

Woven stole (shown in color). Space dyed handspun yarns.

BARBARA L. ANDERSON • Urbana, Illinois

Dog Hair Pillows
Woven Stole
Crocheted Shawl
Weed Bag
"Brown Ripples"

EQUIPMENT DESCRIPTION

The enthusiastic spinner is usually not satisfied with one piece of spinning equipment; and with the large variety of devices available today, sooner or later they manage to have two or three gadgets to do different jobs. I use three different types and I'm still not satisfied! A lovely 100-year-old Canadian flax wheel was my first initiation and it remains my pride and joy. The wheel was originally designed to spin flax and very fine wool yarn, but since I was primarily interested in spinning a medium weight wool, I soon began having problems. Overspin was a constant annoyance and in order to get the wool to wind onto the bobbin, the tension had to be set quite high. This made for difficult treadling and slowed production considerably. Reluctant to give up on the wheel, I did some serious study.

Paula Simmons' *Spinning and Weaving With Wool* offered the best explanation of conquering overspin and it became obvious that the low ratio between the diameter of my bobbin pulley and the drive pulley was the source of the problem. A clever friend fashioned a large drive pulley and it's been easier spinning ever since. Subsequent correspondence with Mrs. Simmons confirmed the value of that decision!

Good wheels being manufactured today are finely tuned machines, but the old wheels have a charm all their own, and if all the pieces are there, if the wheel isn't warped, AND if you know clever people, there's nothing like spinning on a century-old machine that conveys a romance and history unique in contemporary life.

A simple Navajo spindle has provided me with a large quantity of nice bulky yarn. The low cost and portability of the device is very attractive and a couple of hours of determined effort get you spinning quite efficiently. The usual technique is to rest the spindle on your right thigh and roll it along as you pull out the fibers with your left hand. Another technique was shown to me and involves turning the spindle with your right hand, allowing it to stand on the floor, and pulling out the wool with the left hand. This is the method I have used. Periodically the spun fiber is wound onto the shaft. When working with a long fiber, carding is usually not necessary. Short cuts and debris can be plucked out during teasing, and if you have a nice tidy fleece, long narrow sections can be pulled off and quickly prepared for spinning.

A bag of wool and your Navajo spindle can be tucked into a corner of the car and taken on vacations, and of course, for

Photograph by Karl Runkle
Detail of dark pillow worked in loop stitch.

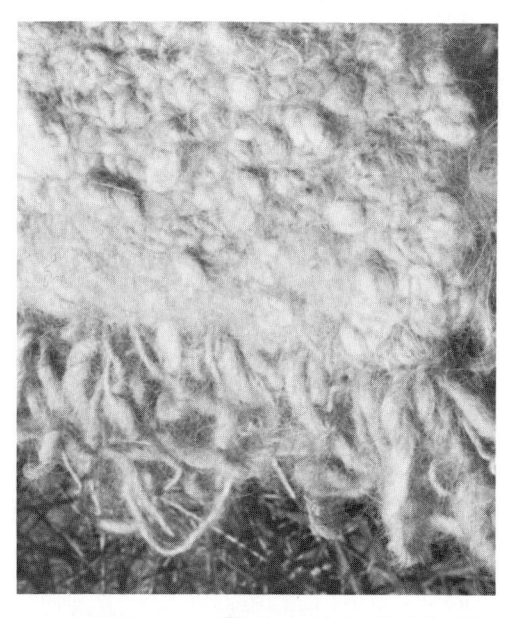

Photograph by Karl Runkle
Detail of beige pillow.

Wool source:
Hedgehog Equipment
Forest Craft Center
Upper Hartfield, East Sussex, England

demonstrations, space needs are minimal. People are always intrigued by this ancient form of spinning fibers.

The new jumbo spinner heads available are all the same basic design, with a variety of bases. Mine is a head mounted on an old treadle sewing machine and despite its odd appearance, does a good job of spinning bulky weight yarn. The one-inch orifice allows for easy draw and the huge bobbin will hold up to two pounds of yarn. The treadling is effortless and production is fast; however, minor problems need to be worked out. When mounting the head on a base like mine, some trial and error is necessary to achieve desirable results. A leather sewing machine belt is used to connect the head to the iron wheel beneath the machine. This belt eventually stretches and needs to be adjusted periodically. The device is heavy and really not appropriate for toting to demonstrations or meetings, but it is a very useful machine in the spinner's workshop.

DOG HAIR PILLOWS

Spinning dog hair is an experience every spinner should have, and asking friends to save dog combings will result in a variety of free fibers. Texture and length will determine how any particular breed's hair is best handled. English Sheepdog hair for example, is long and coarse enough to be spun by itself; soft and fine hair from other breeds works better combined with wool. Using dog combings alone or together with wool, card gently, removing any matts, foreign debris or short pieces. Spin into a medium weight single-ply fiber. Wash skeins in warm, soapy water, hang and weight until dry. For a small pillow (a 14-inch square), you will need about 6-8 ounces of dog hair and a size G or H crochet hook. Select a stitch pattern that produces a closely worked fabric and some textural surface interest. When piece is completed, fold in half, sew two sides closed, stuff until plump with polyester fiberfill and sew remaining edge shut. If fringe is desired, wind yarn around an 8-inch piece of cardboard. Cut one end. With 5 strands together, fold in half, pull loop through edges and tighten knot. Fringe can be as dense as desired, and can be attached on all four sides if you like. Trim evenly.

The beige pillow is crocheted of handspun dog hair from our Bernadette, a large wooly beastie of uncertain parentage. Her hair is long and coarse, ranging from creamy white to varying shades of beige. The following pattern yielded a heavy, soft fabric with an interesting nubbly surface effect.

Foundation chain; Chain 59 and work 1 sc in 2nd ch from hook and in each ch to end. Ch 1, turn.
1st row: 1 sc in 1st sc, * ch 4, 1 sc in each of next 4 sc; rep from *, ending with ch 4, 1 sc in last sc. Ch 1, turn.
2nd row: Holding ch 4 at back (right side), work 1 sc in each sc to end. Ch 1, turn.
3rd row: 1 sc in each of 1st 3 sc, * ch 4, 1 sc in each of next 4 sc; rep from *, ending ch 4, 1 sc in each of last 3 sc. Ch 1, turn.
4th row: Same as row 2. Repeat from row 1 for pattern, and con-

A Complete Guide to Crochet Stitches
Mary M. Dawson

Mon Tricot Knitting and Crochet Dictionary

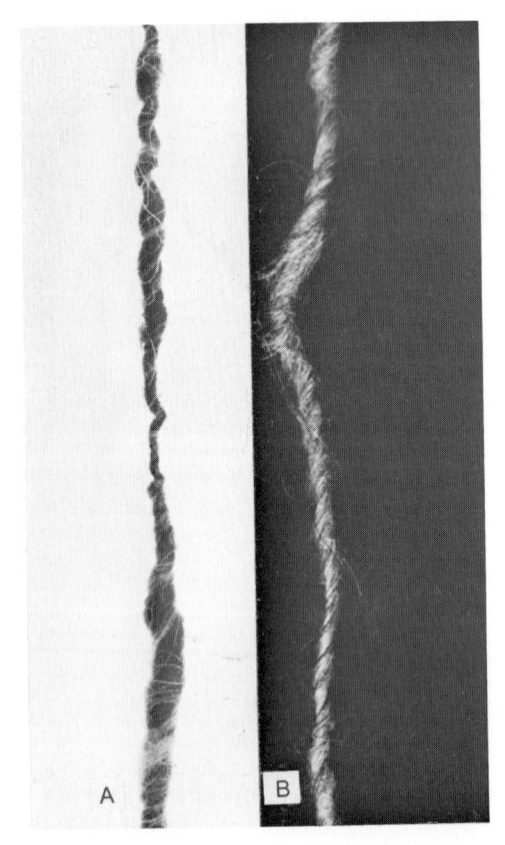

A Huskie-Shepherd hair carded with black wool.

B Bernadette's hair.

tinue for about 12-13 inches. This makes about a 22" wide piece. If a larger pillow is desired, increase the length of the foundation chain, having the total number of chains a multiple of 4 + 3.

The black-beige pillow was crocheted from a mixture of natural black fleece and combings from a pale beige Huskie-Shepherd mixture. The dog hair was very soft, but short and fly-away, so carding it with wool seemed to be the best solution for ease of handling. The yarn was spun into a medium weight single-ply fiber with the dog hair creating a slubby effect. It is strong enough for knitting and crocheting, but would probably not work for warp on a foot-powered loom.

I crocheted a rectangle, alternating rows of single and double crochet with rows of a loop stitch. The loop row was worked at 2-inch intervals, since the fiber was in short supply. A good crochet stitch "dictionary" is invaluable to the handspinner, since many different effects can be obtained with handspun fibers, depending on the pattern used.

WOVEN STOLE

The woven stole is a sample of dye experiments with handspun wool, combined with commercial yarns. My dyeing techniques don't always follow the rule book but I get some beautiful results and no two batches are ever the same. Using two skeins of bulky wool spun on the Navajo spindle, and a couple of skeins of medium weight single-ply wool spun on the Canadian wheel, I put them into the dye pot dry and sprinkled alternate layers with two colors of Cushing dyes; in this case Aqua Green and Violet. The dye pot was carefully filled with tap water so as not to disturb the arrangement. After simmering for about an hour, the result was a beautiful blend of light and medium lavenders, with a slightly greenish cast. Another skein of medium weight yarn was dyed with Putnam's Navy Blue, but only allowed to sit in the dye pot in hot tap water for an hour or so. The result was a bluish lavender.

The yarns seemed to lend themselves to combining with some commercial yarns I had accumulated in a variety of oyster-gray shades. The 4-harness loom was warped 28 inches wide with 3 different threads of these oyster-gray tones at 6 ends per inch. The warp threads consisted of 2 textured boucle wools and one thread of a synthetic-wool blend. I wove the stole 80 inches long in a plain tabby weave, in alternating bands of the dyed handspun yarns and the same yarns used in the warp. Fringe was tied on both ends. The result is a soft garment of muted lavender gray tones. The dyeing technique of layering the wool, sprinkling with dye powders of one color, putting in another layer of wool, adding another color in the same range, can yield some exquisitely beautiful blends. By not wetting the wool first, you have a better chance of getting more clear-cut distinction in color. When dyeing unspun fleece, the dye pot should be watched carefully to avoid extreme temperatures. I set the burner on medium in all cases, to avoid damaging the wool.

Dye source:
W. Cushing & Company
Kennebunkport, Maine 04046

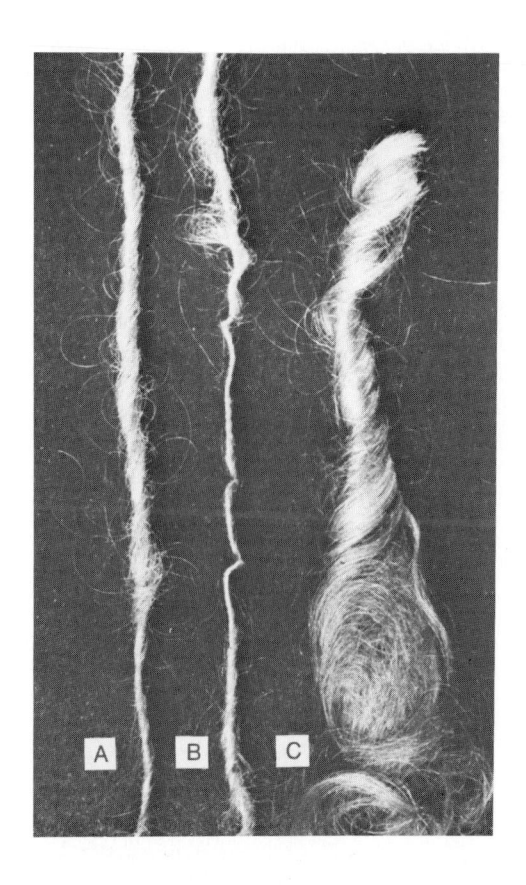

A, B Wool, spun on wheel.

C Wool, spun on Navajo spindle.

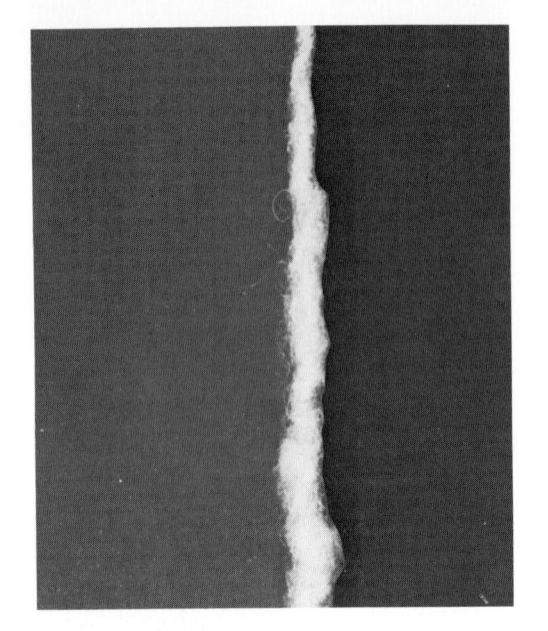

Never agitate unspun fleece in the dye pot, and avoid stirring spun wool if you want the different colors to remain reasonably distinct. Dyeing your handspun bulky yarns with this technique will reward you with some unique fibers that rival the expensive space-dyed commercial yarns available now.

CROCHETED SHAWL

Within a few weeks of acquiring my first spinning wheel, I had accumulated a number of skeins of handspun yarn, some of them more properly spun than others, but nonetheless enough for a big project. A lacy triangular shawl was my choice, something I had long wanted for personal use; and what the yarn lacked in professional quality, was compensated for by the uniqueness of the fiber. I preferred to crochet the shawl, although a knitted shawl pattern would have posed no problems. After researching a number of pattern books, I found a design that seemed appropriate. The pattern called for regular

Wool, crocheted stole.

Detail of crocheted shawl.

Photograph by Karl Runkle

Crocheted shawl, handspun wool, commercial pattern.

knitting worsted and indicated the size hook required to achieve the correct gauge. After some experimentation, a hook one size smaller appeared to be the best choice. A pattern gauge will tell you that a certain number of stitches makes an inch, and a certain number of rows makes an inch. When substituting handspun fibers for commercially spun yarns, checking out the proper stitch gauge is essential. If your four stitches for example don't make an inch with the size hook or needles called for in the pattern, use a larger one. If your sample gauge swatch comes out larger than what is suggested, use a smaller hook or needles. For a garment like a shawl or stole, careful fit is not necessary, but for sweaters or jackets, proper stitch gauge is critical if you want a good fit.

This particular shawl measures 75 inches along the longest edge and took about one and a half pounds of medium weight handspun yarn. Fringe was knotted on two sides and the shawl was washed in warm soapy water and blocked. The shawl is an attractive accessory with a long dress and never fails to draw compliments. Pattern books are full of crocheted and knitted shawls and a little experimenting with hook or needle size should enable you to fashion a memorable garment from your handspun yarn.

WEED BAG

Weed or twig bags are good small projects for the spinner, since odds and ends of different fibers, colors, and weights of yarn can be combined into a unified whole. The bags can be woven, crocheted, or knitted and embellished with beads, feathers, or other natural objects. They make interesting wall accents and are an unusual gift item.

The sample shown is a crocheted rectangle measuring 9 inches by 18 inches. Single crochet was used along with a few rows of loop stitch. Thinner yarns were used double and heavier yarns were saved for fringe and embellishment. In this bag I have used a variety of wool breeds in white, gray, and black.

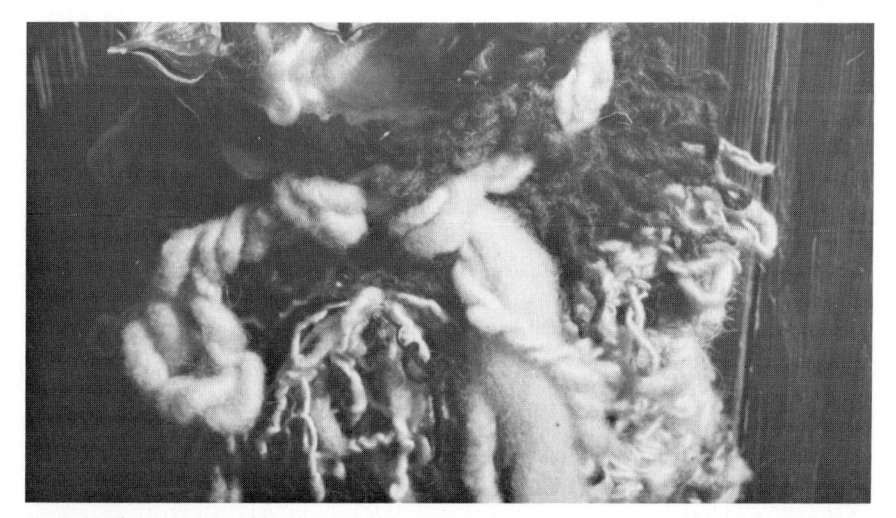

Photograph by Karl Runkle

Weed bag.

Photograph by Karl Runkle

Detail of weed bag.

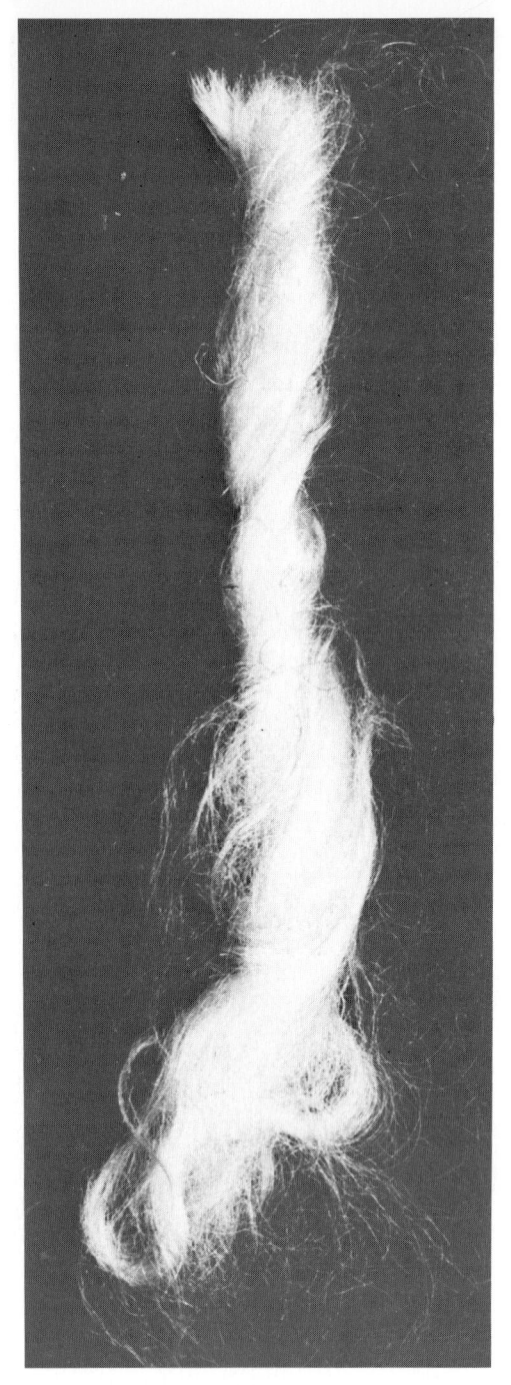

Cotswold, Navajo spindle.

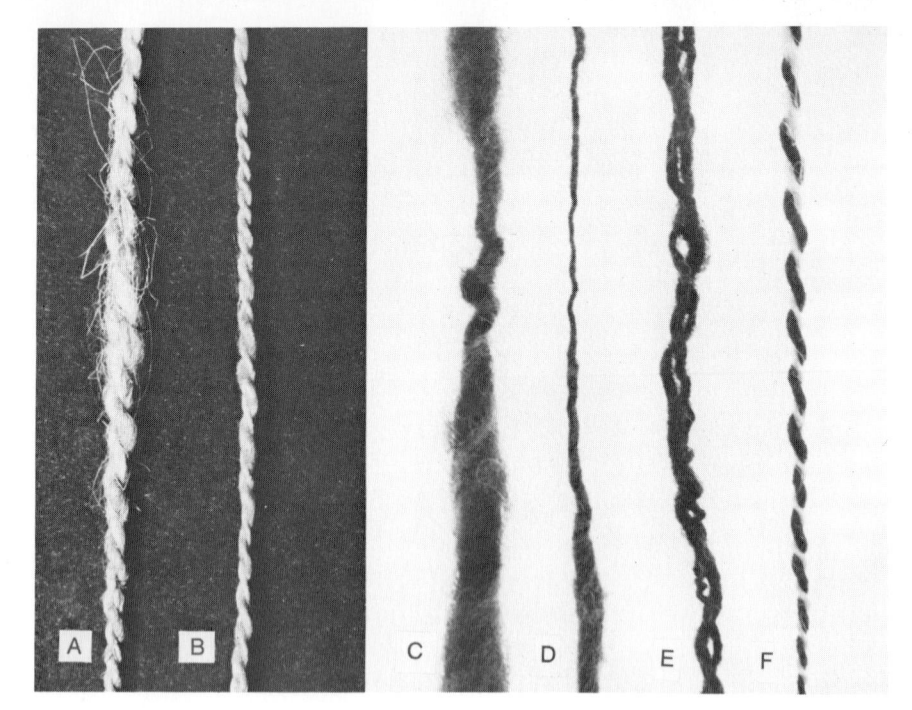

A "Rough Fell," English breed, spun on wheel.
B Wool.
C Wool, Navajo spindle.
D Wool, New Zealand.
E Two ply, black/grey wool, Vermont.
F Cotswold and Black Masham, 2 ply, wheel.

The rectangle was folded over with the edges meeting in the middle, and strands of fringe were knotted through both edges down the center. The bottom was stitched closed. To draw the bag in at the top, bulky yarn was laced through a row about an inch from the edge and knotted in front. A small plastic or metal ring can be sewn on the back for hanging. I like to stuff the bags with a handful of clean unspun fleece to plump them out. Poke a hole into the fleece for the dried materials and it's finished! The same procedure can be used for a knitted rectangle, or a piece woven on a frame or cardboard loom. Of course, who says it has to be a rectangle?

"BROWN RIPPLES"

"Brown Ripples" is a crocheted wall piece composed of a variety of yarns and mounted on a copper tube. Handspun bulky yarn is featured in some surface interest and fringe. A very ordinary skein of cream-brown-gray commercial knitting worsted inspired the combination of other brown, off-white, and gray textured yarns. The handspun used is a brown-gray shaded fleece spun on the jumbo spinner head. The basic pattern used is the familiar "ripple" afghan stitch, and lends itself beautifully to incorporating loop stitch techniques, crocheted "ruffles" on the surface, and chained stitch loops of the bulky yarn worked on the basic piece. The general pattern follows:

> For a piece about 14 inches wide that will have 3 large points, begin by chaining 85 stitches.
> Row 1: 1 sc in 2nd ch from hook, *(ch 1, skip 1 ch, 1 sc in next ch) 6 times; ch 1, skip 1 ch, in next chain work (1 sc and ch 1) 3 times for an increase group (top of point), (ch 1, skip 1 ch, sc in next ch) 6 times; skip 3 ch, repeat from * across row, ending in the last ch. Ch 2, turn.

Row 2: Skip first sc, *(sc in next sc, ch 1) 6 times, work an inc group in center sc of previous inc group, (ch 1, sc in next sc) 6 times, skip 2 sc, repeat from * across row. Ch 2, turn. Repeat row 2 for desired length.

To make a more open row for lacing heavy yarns through, substitute double crochet for single crochet. The loop stitch technique can also be substituted for the single crochet. The surface ruffles are simple to do and are very effective. These kinds of embellishments can be added when the piece is finished. To make the ruffles, select a row where you have done a double crochet instead of a single crochet. Loop the end of the yarn to be used around the "leg" of the first double crochet on a row, and make a loop on the hook. Make 2 or 3 chains and single crochet around the "leg" of the next double crochet. Continue across the row. Chain 3, turn, and work at least five double crochets into each ch-3 loop across the whole row. The more stitches packed into this little loop, the fuller the ruffle will be. A ruffle can have as many rows added to it as you desire. Treble or double treble stitches can also be used to make a longer ruffle.

The handspun bulky yarn was woven through rows of double crochet and was also used in the chaining technique, using a large hook and picking up the "legs" of the double crochet foundation stitches with 3 or 4 chains between each one. The yarn was so fat, this was sufficient for a good 3-dimensional effect.

Your imagination must be your guide here, and as the piece takes shape, more ideas will occur to you for additional textural interest. Fringe can be knotted anywhere and is a must along the bottom of the piece. For the mounting rod, I purchased a length of half-inch copper tubing at the hardware store and cut it about 14 inches long. Our store had little copper end caps to fit each tip. The piece was attached to the rod for hanging. The copper color blended nicely with the brown tones in the wall hanging. This basic pattern can be expanded to make larger hangings or full-size afghans. I have also adapted it to a stole, simply making the basic chain proportionately longer. Try a small piece first and then let yourself go!

Photograph by Karl Runkle
"Brown Ripples" crocheted wall hanging.

Detail of "Brown Ripples."

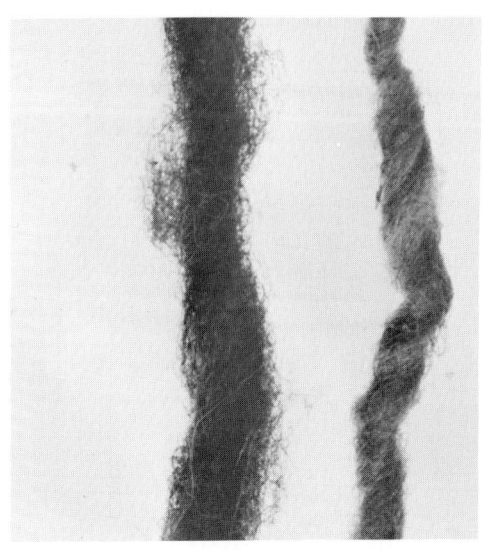

"Brown Ripples."

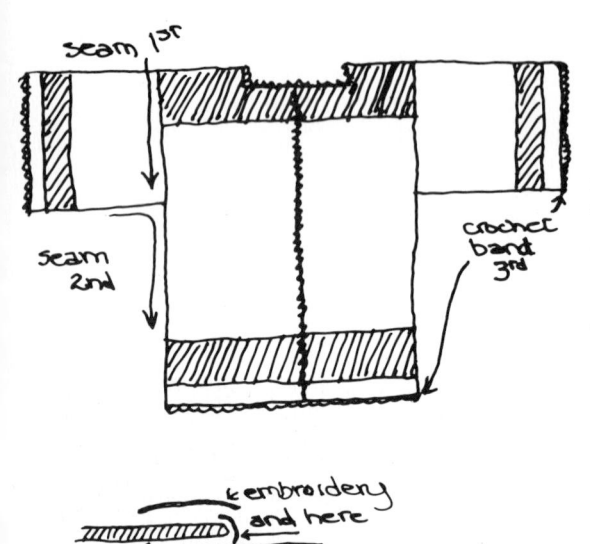

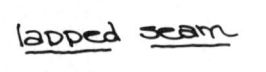

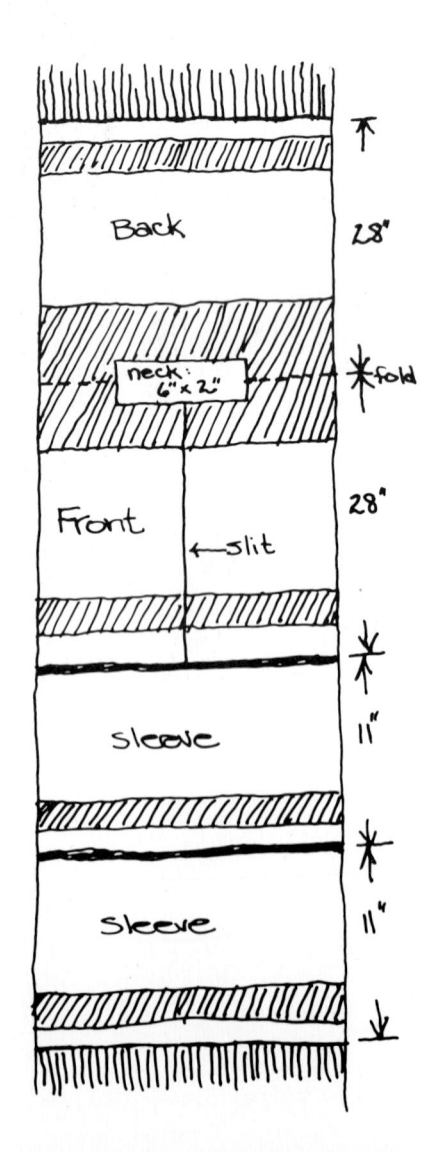

CAROL MARSH HOBDAY • Westfield, Massachusetts
Kimono Jacket

KIMONO JACKET

A friend provided a prize Merino fleece for the weft of this garment. The wool was not especially dirty, so it was possible to card and spin in the grease, that is, without washing the wool first. The spinning wheel used was an Ashford. A single ply, fairly heavy weight yarn seemed to show off the beautiful lustre of the Merino fiber best. For warp I used a commercially available 2 ply yarn blended of wool, nylon and angora. It saved quite a bit of spinning time and provided a finer warp.

Most of the jacket was woven of the natural colored wool on the natural colored warp. For the contrasting stripes, four harmonious shades of natural colors made a subtle but rich contrast. The two darker shades are the result of using onion skins as the dyestuff with chrome and alum mordants. The two yellow shades come from broom sedge, a grassy plant found along roads everywhere. Again, chrome and alum were used as mordants. Both are good dyestuffs, especially in winter, as they are commonly available year round.

Originally this jacket was intended as an entry in a show with the theme "Till Spring", to keep a body warm, till spring! The construction is a very old, simple style, very comfortable and cozy to wear. No cutting was necessary as there is very little fitting involved in a garment of this sort. Rectangles of cloth directly from the loom were hand sewn together using a decorative embroidery stitch to emphasize the single seams. The extreme simplicity of the style highlights the beauty of the cloth, while the simplicity of the weave shows off the yarn. To lend stability to the edges of the garment — since it will be worn a lot — a banding of crochet was added along all edges, using the warp yarn dyed with onion skins. The placement of the stripes emphasized the relationship of the jacket to the human body. The only problem encountered in the weaving process was the sett of the warp yarns in relation to the size of the handspun, to avoid a cloth that was either too weak or too stiff. This was easily solved by making a series of samples at different setts. This also aided greatly in the calculations of amounts of yarn to spin and dye. The resulting sett was 12 ends of warp to the inch set in the tabby threading on a 25" four harness floor loom. I used a 10 dent reed with every fifth dent doubled. This caused a subtle striping effect that I found pleasing. Weaving width was 22" with some take-up during weaving and during later washing. This jacket was a first for this spinner in that the entire project was planned in advance, including amounts to spin and amounts to dye for the stripes.

Kimono jacket. Natural dyes are broom sedge and onion skins. Shown in color.

Photograph by Grenier-Ducharme Photography

Merino, singles.

Working from my sample, I settled upon 10 weft shots per inch, to be on the generous side. Total woven area was 22" by 78".

```
        24" w (some take up allowed)
       x 10  shots per inch
        240" of weft used per inch of cloth
       x 78" woven
     18,720" or 520 yds of weft needed
```

My filled spinning wheel bobbins were measuring 55 yds, so I spun 12 bobbins. I dyed one each of 4 colors, leaving 8 natural. I had loads.

Figuring out the warp yardage was even easier:

```
    78"  weaving
     6"  spaces between pieces
    30"  knots and waste
    20"  take-up
   134"  or 4 yards warped
    24"  weaving width
  x 10   threads per inch
   240   total threads
   x 4   yards of warp
   960   yards of warp (about 1/3 pound
         of this particular yarn)
```

For reference material, I used *Weaving You Can Wear* as a jumping off point and modified one of Jean Wilson's layouts to be more like a knitted sweater I have.

Photograph by Grenier-Ducharme Photography
Close-up of kimono jacket showing detail of weave, shoulder seam.

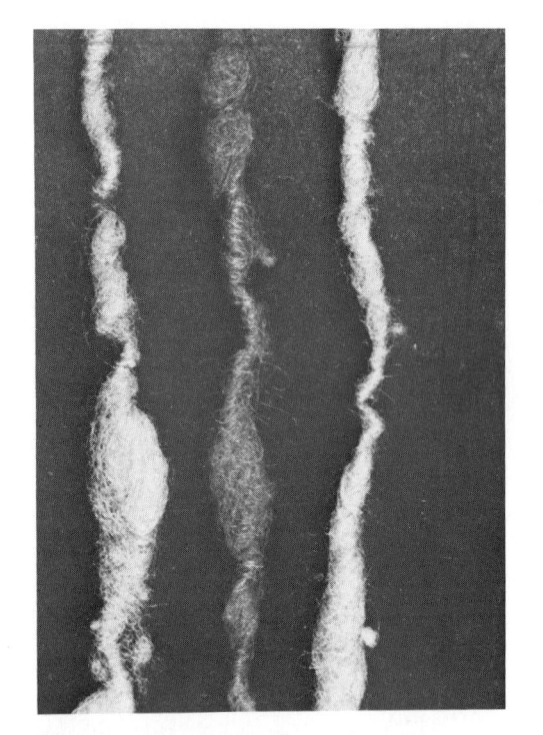

DEBORAH DAW • Cambridge, Massachusetts
Björknäs Harvest, 3' by 6', linen warp, wool weft, oats and wheat stalks

I spent the summer of 1976 with friends on their farm in Sweden, watching the fields ripen. The array of golden hues as the wheat and oats matured inspired this hanging, which I left behind as a thank you present.

The fleece was purchased from a local distributor. I used Gobelins (a quality of fleece named after the famous tapestry weaving factory) and also local fleece. The dyes are all from plant matter I collected on the farm.

After a thorough washing, I carded the Gobelins and local wool together. I decided to card them together because the Gobelins was of such superior quality that I wanted to make a good thing last! It made spinning easier and the resultant yarn was softer and more lustrous. Half of the yarn I spun before dyeing, the rest after dyeing. I worked solely on a drop spindle, spinning a coarse, slubby yarn essential to the textured surface I wanted to achieve on the hanging. I also plyed colors together and used some dyed fleece in its unspun state.

All dyes were obtained from plant matter at Björknäs, mordanting only with alum and chrome. Every plant yielded brilliant colors, with the exception of the lily of the valley leaves, which should be harvested in spring, rather than at midsummer.

Björknäs Harvest was woven on a home-constructed Salish frame (plans from *The Off-Loom Weaving Book*). It was warped at approximately 10 epi. The design is simple and primitive — to allow for play with color and texture. The colors arranged themselves; lighter shades for the sun and more mellow shades for the undulating fields below. The principal weave is twining,

Gobelins carded with local (Swedish) fleece, naturally dyed.

Björknäs Harvest shown in color; see front pages.

The Off-Loom Weaving Book
Rose Naumann and Raymond Hull

in the tradition of Salish blankets. Twining is an old weave, used most proficiently by our own Northwest Salish Indians in their blankets. The weaver works with a doubled-over strand of weft and twists these ends by crossing them in front of every warp string. Thus both front and back of the warp are covered. I also left some open areas wherein stalks of oats and wheat were inserted and held in place with Elmer's glue, which dries invisibly when used sparingly.

Some old Swedish books were used for reference and also the knowledge of weavers Carin Cluer and her mother Kerstin Åkestrom.

Dye Recipes

Plant	Comments	Quantity of Dyeplant Material	Quantity of Wool Treated with alum	Quantity of Wool Treated with chrome
Coreopsis	freshly picked flowers	100 grams*	25 grams (gold)	25 grams
Birch leaves	green, dried	100 grams	25 grams (gold)	25 grams (green gold)
Rock lichen	dried lichen I scraped from trees yielded a dull, nothing color	100 grams	25 grams	25 grams (copper)
Lily of the valley leaves	mature, freshly picked	100 grams	25 grams	25 grams (dark gold)
Apple leaves	freshly picked	100 grams	25 grams (gold)	25 grams (brilliant gold)

*about 4 ounces

ODESSA VASQUEZ • Los Osos, California
White Bedspread
Striped Bedspread with Handspun Warp
Bag in Bound Weave
Hanging

WHITE BEDSPREAD

After I learned to spin a smooth yarn consistently, I wanted to use the yarn in something of lasting value, so I decided to weave a bedspread. I wanted it to be entirely my own, so I started to spin the yarn to determine the size and amounts it would need. It took a lot of planning and figuring. I decided I would have to use commercial cotton warp as I had not perfected cotton spinning. A 10/2 natural cotton set at 24 epi proved to be right with my handspun wool, whereas 30 epi was a bit too close.

The pattern I chose was an original one. Years ago in an adult education class taught by Mary Snyder in Pasadena, California, we were given an assignment to combine a star or rose, circle and table in overshot weave, adding a border. The draft which resulted from this study was used for the bedspread.

The wool used was purchased from a rancher at Timber Cove, California in Sonoma County. It was a Romney fleece

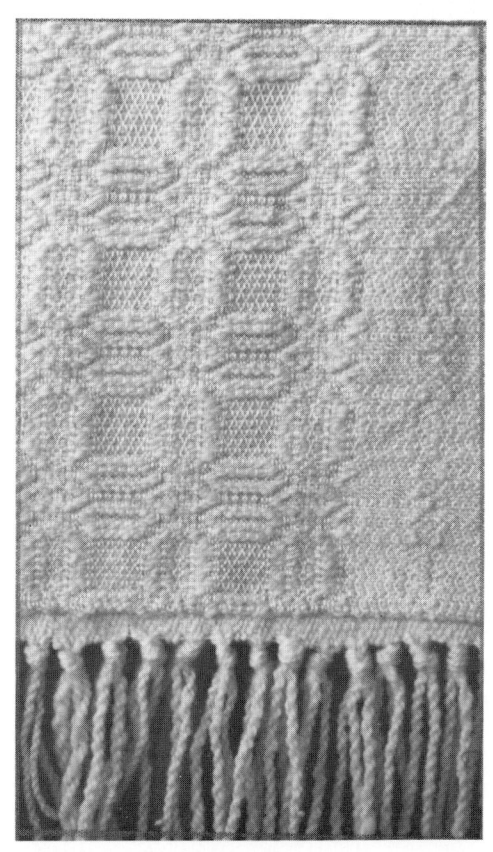

Detail of white bedspread. Handspun wool weft, handspun linen tabby.

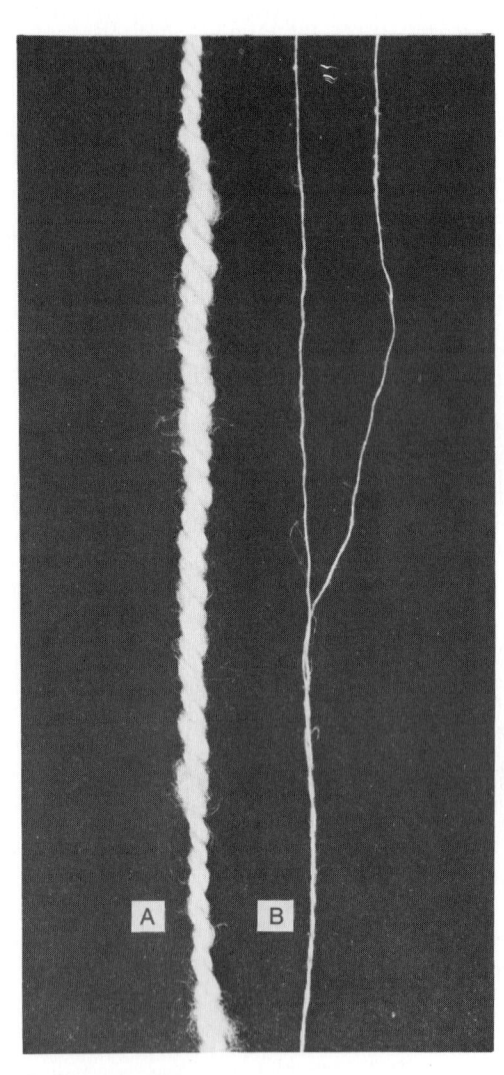

A Two ply, Romney.
B Two ply, flax.

and had to be skirted (sorted) before use. The fleece was laid in a tub of hot water, but not hotter than my hands could stand, without soap or detergent. This water removed all dirt and sand, but not the oil. It was carefully lifted out of the water and placed into mesh bags or pillow slips which were placed into a washer and spun to remove the water. Then it was spread out on a sheet in the driveway to dry. The fleece weighed about 10 pounds. There was a loss of over 40%, yielding about 6 pounds of spun yarn before the final washing. Six pounds of wool yarn were used in weaving and for the fringe.

Next came hours of teasing and hand carding. The yarn was spun on an Ashford wheel, then plied, spinning reverse, which took out any slight overspin and made a lovely soft, silky yarn. Skeins were made and washed well in washing soda and Ivory Liquid detergent and rinsed several times (taking care that water temperatures didn't vary). I added a water softener to the final rinse. Several skeins were washed at a time and then dried on an expanding skein winder. I find that the yarn dries with no kinks when stretched on a skein winder rather than hanging on a line with weights.

For the tabby, natural flax was finely spun and plied in two ply. A wet sponge was used to dampen fingers while spinning the flax. The skeins were washed to set the ply.

The spread was woven on a 40", 4 harness jack loom. It was woven in two strips with a seam in the center. Eight yards of warp were used, making each strip 3½ yards long, which relaxed after washing to 3 yards. The finished spread was 80" wide by 108" long, plus 4" fringe.

Wanting a fringe, but not wanting it to fray or mat as handspun is apt to do when it is washed, I experimented with sample fringes and came up with the following process: I set up a heading 1" wide with the 10/2 cotton (2 ends per heddle used as one). Eight inches to the left a very heavy cord was put through the reed but not through a heddle. The whole chain of heavy cord was the same length as the heading warp — 11 yards — and was tied to the front tie rod, but not to the warp beam. The heavy cord was hung over the back beam and weighted with a heavy weight — an old 5 pound sash weight — (wonderful the uses for old fashioned things around a weaving studio). My idea was to weave a fringe that would not need to be cut at the ends. The single spun wool yarn was respun much tighter, washed to set the twist and wound into balls to keep it from twisting back on itself. The weaving of fringe was as follows: Weave through the heading, around the cord, back into heading. Change shed, through heading only, change shed, back through heading. Change shed and weave through heading and around cord, back through heading. The beater does not need to be used as the shuttle or fingers can press the wool into place. When finished, the cord was cut (back of reed) and the fringe slipped off. As each end came off it plied back on itself. Three plied strands of fringe were knotted together in an overhand knot at the heading. The heading was hand stitched to sides and foot of the spread. The spread was then washed in a bathtub in warm water and mild detergent (Ivory Liquid again), rinsed, water spun out in the washing machine and then hung outside on the clothesline to dry in the breeze. Finally, I took it to the dry cleaner for steam pressing. The fringe is lovely, and stands washing without tangling.

STRIPED BEDSPREAD WITH HANDSPUN WARP

The San Luis Obispo County Fair in Paso Robles, California was landscaped with beds and beds of beautiful gold, yellow and orange marigolds. The gardener was cleaning and thinning them before the fair opened and gladly gave me trash barrels of the flowers. What a gold mine! I had many pounds of white New Zealand Romney wool spun for some project. I visualized a striped bedspread for my husband's bed. Out came the dye pots! Three days were spent with alum and cream of tartar for mordant, stannous chloride added to some; copper sulphate to some, chrome to some. The colors that emerged were beautiful, blended and compatible. The stripes were arranged by winding yarn around an old venetian blind slat and counting the number in each stripe. An 8 dent reed was tried and the yarn cleared without sticking. No sizing was used, but it probably would have been helpful. The handspun yarn was wound on a warping reel in the following rotation:

  2 — 2 ply natural brown
 10 — old gold
  8 — yellow
  2 — brown
  4 — orange (yellow with small amount cochineal)
 16 — gold
  2 — brown
  4 — orange
  4 — brown
  8 — old gold
  2 — brown

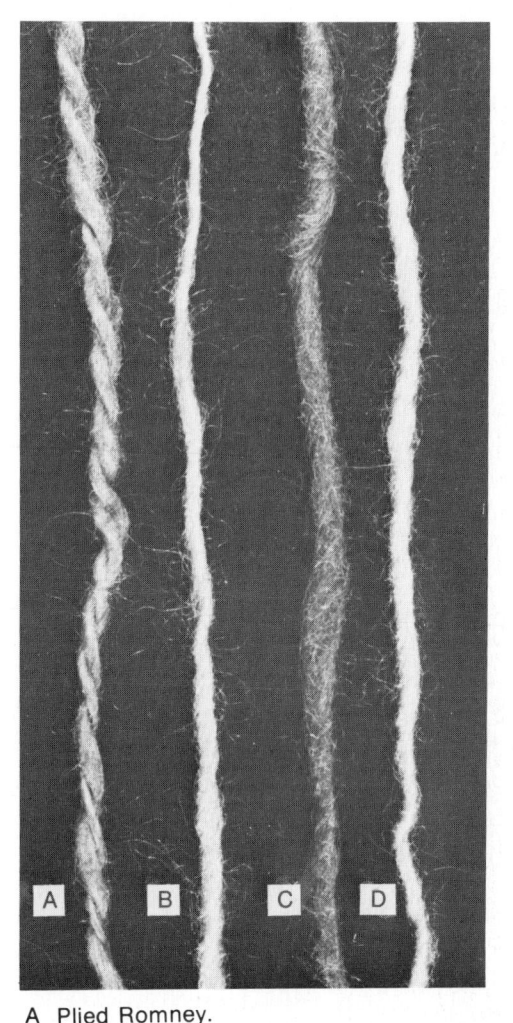

A Plied Romney.
B, C, D New Zealand Romney.

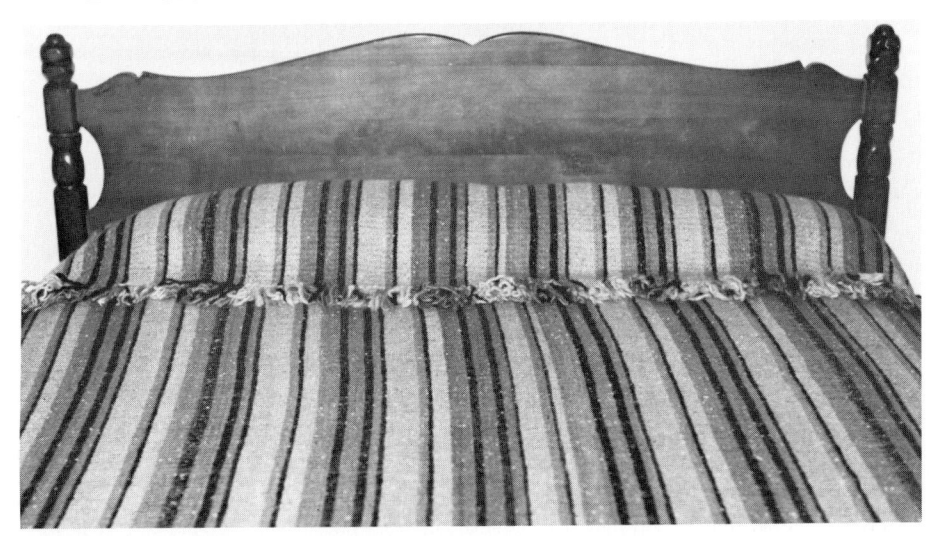

Striped bedspread, handspun naturally dyed warp. Seams concealed in two of the dark stripes.

Detail of bag, showing square knotted shoulder strap.

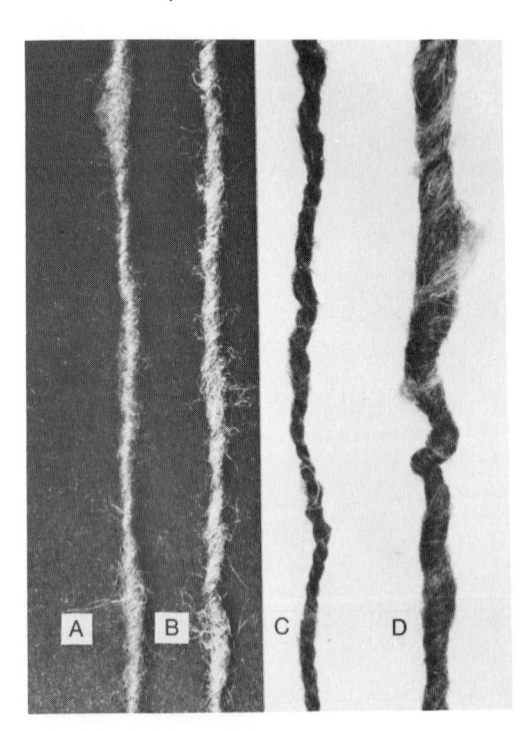

A Singles wool, gray.
B Wool, dyed orange.
C Wool, 2 ply, brown.
D Brown wool mixed with orange flecks of chopped up knitting yarn.

Note: Also see Collie hair used in hanging.

This sequence was repeated 5 times, making a total of 320 ends, in a twill threading, sleyed at 8 epi. The weaving was done in a plain weave using a light brown tweed for the weft. I used a direct tie-up on the loom — one harness tied to one treadle. This made it easier to clear the shed and keep the warp threads from sticking together. I would press treadle 1, then treadle 3, and then, with both harnesses up, throw the shuttle. For the next shed I pressed treadle 2 followed by 4. A stretcher (temple) was used to keep the full width; however, it still relaxed by 2 inches when I took it off the loom. The spread was woven in 3 widths, with the seams in the brown stripes where they didn't show. The ends of the warp through the heddles were left on and knotted for a fringe. The center strip was unraveled for the fringe width. On the bed the pillows lay on the spread and the fringed part folds down over the pillows and shows. The spread was washed after seaming, dried over the line outside, then steamed and pressed by a cleaner. (The clothesline is run through a long piece of white plastic water pipe and fastened tightly. This prevents a crease from forming while the spread dries.)

Finished size after pressing was 108" wide by 120" long. Eight pounds of handspun yarn was used in the warp and 1½ pounds of the commercial tweed yarn in the weft.

BAG IN BOUND WEAVE

This bag is woven in bound weave technique, on a simple overshot pattern. Bound weave is excellent for heavy articles, such as bags, rugs or hangings. The warp must be set far apart — 6 epi for this bag. The warp was a brown 8/4 carpet warp, doubled. A floating selvedge thread (through the last dent of reed but not through a heddle) should be used. The warp is entirely covered.

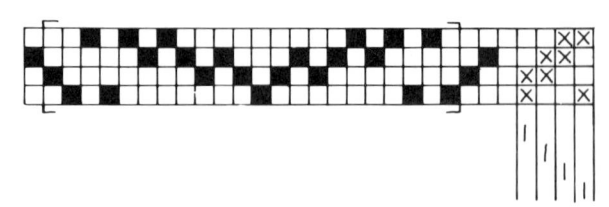

Tension is kept tight. The weft is laid in loosely (arc or bubble it). Treadling is always 1-2, 2-3, 3-4, 4-1. The order never varies. All variations or patterns come from changing the order of the colors of the weft. Beating should be firm, to cover the warp. A hand fork beater can be used if necessary.

Handspun weft yarns were natural brown sheep wool, gray sheep wool, beige collie dog hair and white wool dyed with dollar eucalyptus leaves — making burnt orange.

The bag is lined and a strip of Velcro is used to fasten the top together. The shoulder strap is square knotted with one strand of each weft yarn over a center strand of 2 sisal cords.

The bag was woven on warp 24 inches wide and folded sideways for a 12-inch width.

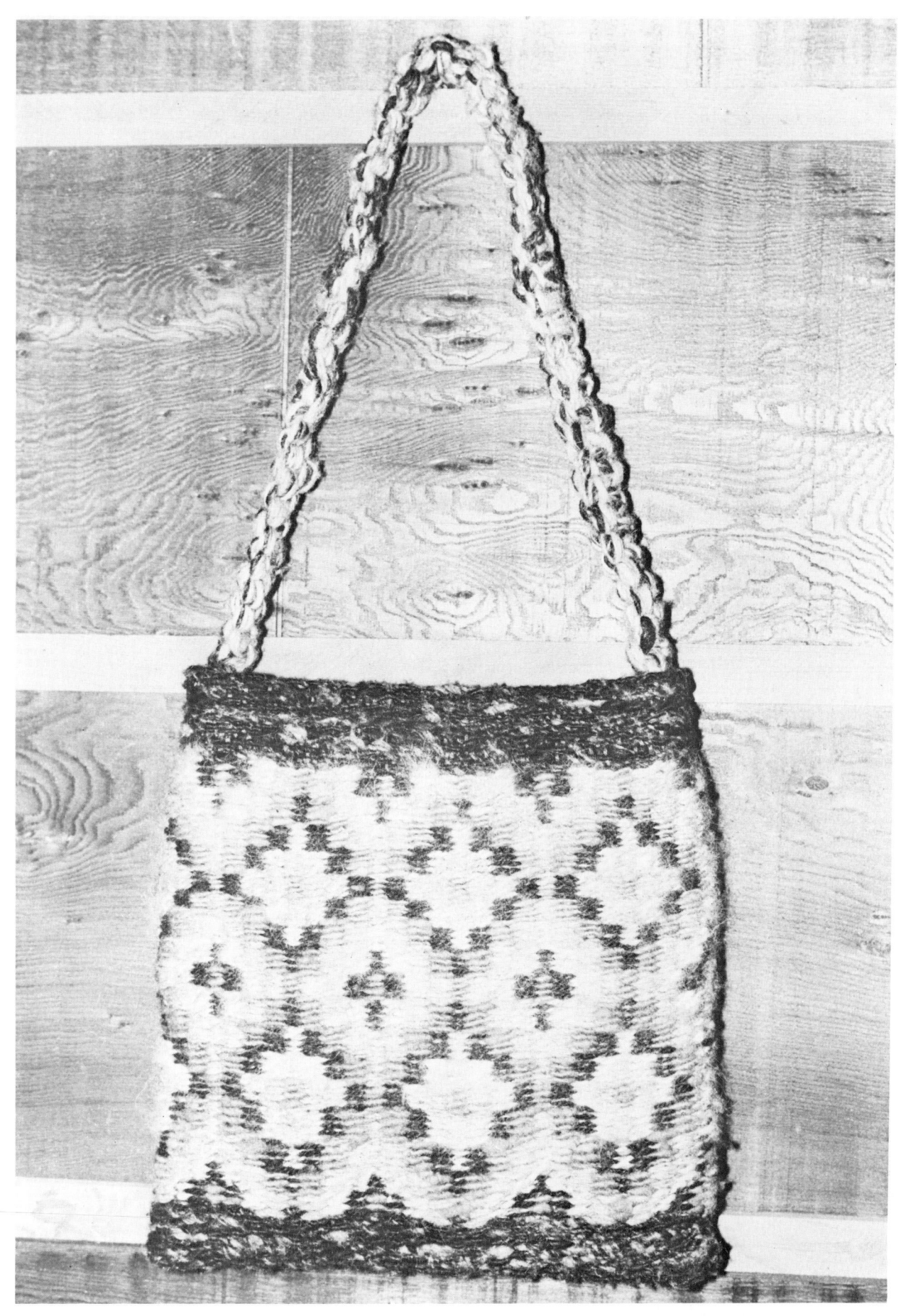

Bag in bound weave. Wool, dog hair.

Hanging, tapestry weave with killim slits.

HANGING
24" x 38"

This design was modified from a picture in an old Handweavers & Craftsman Magazine. The warp is 8/4 cotton carpet warp, sett 8 epi — 200 ends, threaded to twill for plain weave. The handspun weft yarns are New Zealand Romney wool in white, brown and gray. I also used tan collie dog hair. The New Zealand wool was purchased carded but not scoured. There was no waste. It was spun in a smooth, medium twist. The collie hair had been saved by a friend and was mixed, white, brown and tan. In carding, some of each type was put on the cards so that it blended into one soft color. The collie sections have fuzzed slightly giving a very soft effect.

The weaving was tapestry weaving with killim slits. After determining the angle of the design, the number of turns around the warp before advancing or decreasing was calculated to be two. More times made the angle too steep and one made it flat. The thickness of the weft is the determining factor.

This hanging was woven on a 4 harness jack loom, which, of course, left warp fringe ends. The warp ends were inserted back into the web for 1/2 to 3/4 inch with a needle, and then the ends trimmed.

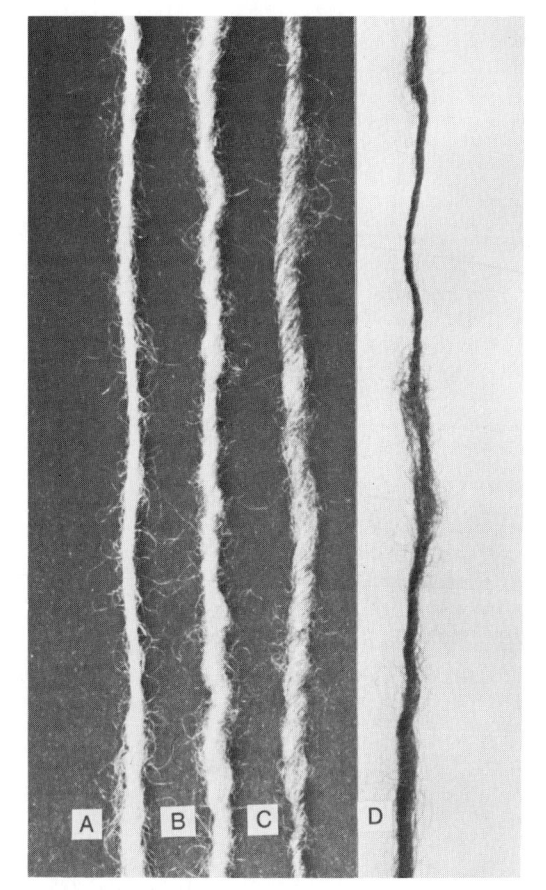

A New Zealand Romney.
B Wool.
C Collie dog hair (also used in bag).
D New Zealand Romney.

Detail of hanging.

FAITH TSUKROFF WILSON • New Haven, Connecticut
JUDY TSUKROFF • Norfolk, Connecticut

GLOVES

The Spinning

I needed and wanted a good-looking, warm pair of gloves and decided to spin the yarn for them myself, both because I enjoy spinning and because I wanted to make something with handspun yarn. I like the natural color of wool and wanted the design on the gloves to be simple with just a few stripes to provide contrast, and because I like stripes.

The gloves are a combination of black Newfoundland dog hair combings and white Cheviot wool. Both wool and dog hair were spun unwashed. The wool was teased, hand-carded, and spun. The dog hair was spun without any processing. After the yarn was spun and plied, the skeins were washed in warm water and Ivory Snow and then boiled. I did this so that the yarn would shrink as much as it was going to. It still retained its elasticity and body.

There were two yarns used in the gloves. One was plain wool, spun and plied on a homemade drop spindle. I spun half the wool with an S-twist and half with a Z-twist and then plied them together in an S-twist to make a 2-ply yarn. The wool and dog hair yarn was made by putting a small amount of wool on a carder and laying an equal amount of dog hair on top and then carding the two together. The spinning and plying were the same as for the wool yarn. Despite spinning the singles fairly thin, the yarn, when plied, was thicker than I had wanted.

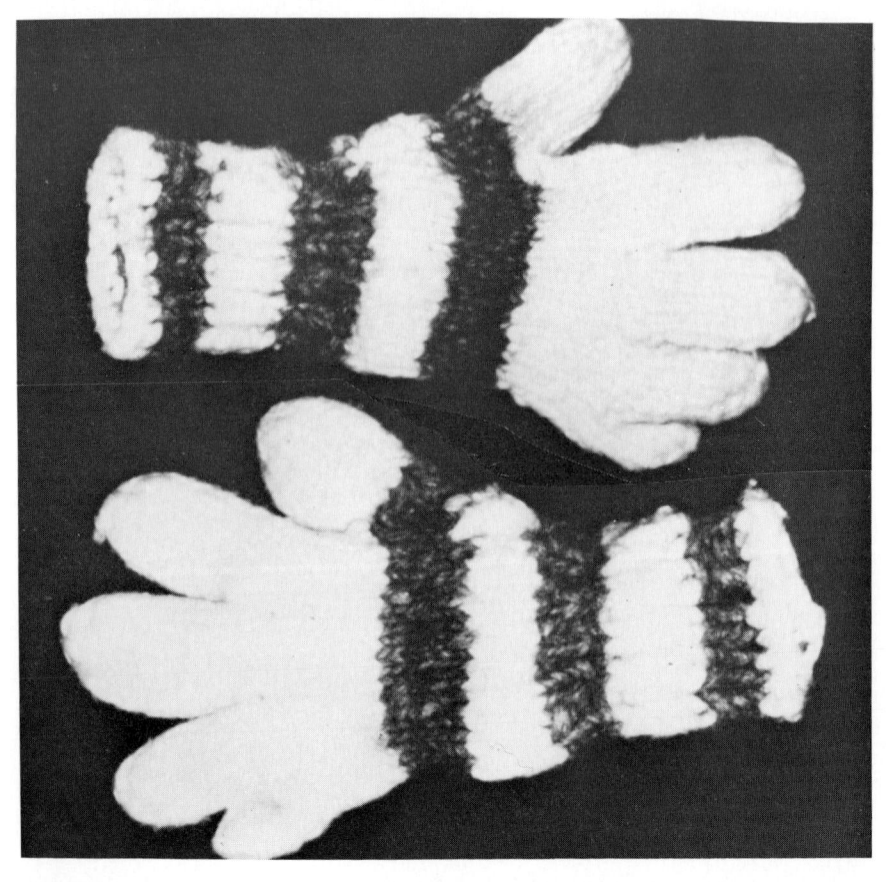

Your Handspinning
Elsie G. Davenport

Knitted gloves, 2 ply yarn.   Photograph by Nathan Tsukroff

Since I first started spinning, I've been interested in mixing other fibers with wool to produce interesting yarns. I've used short rabbit fur and poodle hair as well as the Newfoundland dog hair. I thought it would be interesting to use yarn made with Newfoundland dog hair for the black stripes. I also knew the dog and enjoyed making something using fur from a friend.

My mother, Judy Tsukroff, did the knitting, as I didn't know how.

FAITH TSUKROFF WILSON

The Knitting

This pattern made a pair of gloves for a small woman's hand.

Stitch gauge in *plain knitting* — 4 stitches = 1 inch; 4½ rows = 1 inch. I used a set of four double-pointed needles, probably size 5. Check your own gauge before you begin by knitting 10 or 12 stitches of plain knit for about 2 inches with your yarn. The gauge would probably change ½ stitch for each size needle. I did not use smaller size needles for the ribbing as people usually do because the yarn was bulky and awkward on finer needles. You will also need two stitch holders and a yarn needle.

If you are going to stripe your gloves, divide the yarn for stripes into two almost equal parts. Use the smaller amount for the first glove, so you will be sure to have enough to do the same striping on the second glove. You can design your own stripes if you prefer.

To begin:

Cast on 20 sts of the grey yarn and divide on 3 needles (6, 6, and 8 sts). Work in K1, P1 for 15 rounds: 5 rounds grey, 5 white, and 5 grey.

Then using white yarn K once around. The glove continues in plain knitting. In the 2nd K round inc 1 st in the first st of each needle (7, 7, and 9 sts, total of 23). [I did this after one round of white because the white was stronger than the soft grey yarn and would take any strain better.] K the 3rd round plain.

Round 4: (Begin the thumb gusset) P and K in the 1st st, K1, K and P in the 3rd stitch, and K around. *Round 5:* K around. *Round 6:* K with grey around. *Round 7:* P and K in the first st, K3, then K and P in the next st and K around. *Rounds 8 and 9:* K around. *Round 10:* P and K in the first st, K5, K and P in the next st and K around. *Round 11:* K around (29 sts). [Yes, there are 6 rounds of grey in this stripe because I had enough, and it looked nice.]

Knitting the thumb: Leave the first 9 sts on the 1st needle for the thumb [these are the sts where I did all that increasing for the gusset.] Put the rest of the sts on 1 or 2 st holders (whatever is easiest). Then divide the thumb sts on 2 needles (5 and 4). Using white yarn (from now on) knit them. On a 3rd needle, cast on 2 sts (11 sts total). [I found it easier to knit around by knitting one more stitch, from the next needle, onto my cast-on needle, to distribute the stitches a little more evenly on the 3 needles.] Knit around until the thumb measures 2¼", measuring from the cast-on sts.

To finish thumb: K2 together all around ending with K1. Cut the yarn leaving a 4-inch end. Thread end on a yarn needle and slip through each st as you slip it off the needle. In other words, run the yarn through all the sts — going around in the same direction that you are knitting. Pull the thumb closed and leave the end to finish off later.

Editor's Note:

For more information on knitting gloves from scratch, see *Mary Thomas's Knitting Book* by Mary Thomas.

To K the hand: Arrange the sts from the holders on 3 needles. To begin knitting take the free needle and pick up 3 sts at the base of the thumb. [I always pick up 3 where I had cast on 2, picking up in the convenient holes; before, between, and after the cast-on sts. This leaves less openness between fingers etc. and is more flexible.] Mark the first pickup st as the beginning of the round (23 sts). K around until the hand measures 1½" from the base of the thumb (where sts were picked up). Don't cut yarn. Check mark to make sure that you are at the beginning of the round.

To K fingers on left hand glove: First finger — K the first 6 sts from the beginning of the round and leave them on the needle. Put the next 9 sts on a st holder for the backs of the fingers. On the 2nd holder put the next 6 sts for the fronts. Keep the last 2 sts on the needle, but don't knit them. Use a free needle to cast on 2 sts between the 6 sts and the 2 sts (10 sts). Then knit around, distributing them comfortably on the needles until the finger measures 2½" from the cast-on sts.

To finish finger: K2 tog around, then cut the yarn and run it through the sts as for thumb.

Second finger — Put 3 sts from the back holder on one needle, 2 sts from the front holder on another needle. Using a new needle, pick up 3 sts from the base of the first finger, then K the 2 front sts. Cast on 2 sts, then knit the 3 back sts. K and finish exactly as 2nd finger left hand.

Third finger — Everything is the same as the second finger, except the length, which is 2½" before finishing.

Fourth finger — Put the last sts from the holders on 2 needles, and pick up 3 sts from the base of the third finger (8 sts). Knit the finger 1½", measuring from between the fingers, before finishing.

To knit right hand glove: Knit exactly the same as the first glove up to the fingers.

Right hand fingers: First finger — Check your mark to be sure that you are at the beginning of the round. K 5 sts and leave them on the needle. Put the next 6 sts on a holder for the fronts of the fingers. On the other holder put the next 9 sts for the backs. The last 3 sts are left on their needle. With a free needle cast on 2 sts between the other 2 needles (10 sts). Knit same as the first finger, left hand.

Second finger — Put 3 sts from the back holder on one needle, 2 sts from the front holder on another needle. K this finger exactly as the second finger, left hand.

Third finger — Begin same as second finger, right hand above. Then finish same as left hand, third finger.

Fourth finger — Same as the fourth finger, left hand.

Then try on the gloves. Hopefully all your fingers will be comfortable. It is a hassle to pull out the tips and make them longer or shorter.

To finish finger tips: Pull each yarn end tight. With a yarn needle push each end down inside the finger tip. When they are all inside, turn the gloves inside out. Tack each end once or twice and run it under a couple of sts before cutting close to knitting. For durability you can crochet once around the wrist of the glove with the stronger of your yarns.

JUDY TSUKROFF

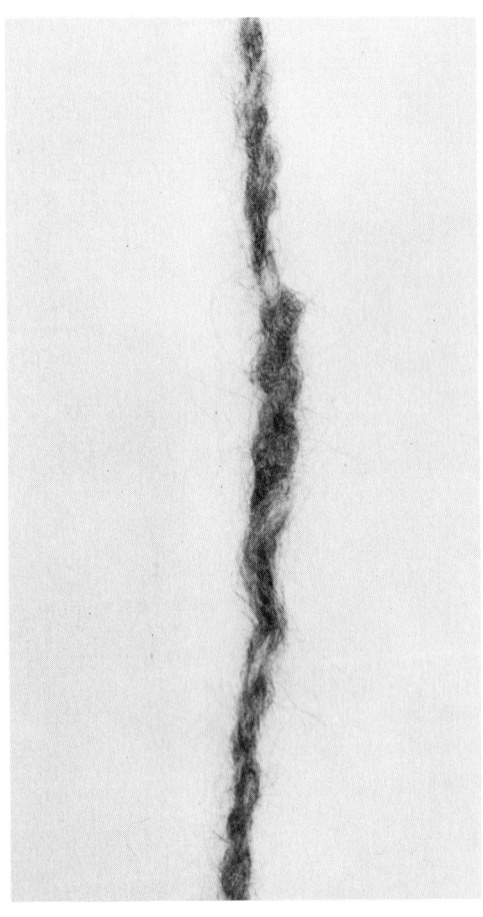

Cheviot wool carded together with Newfoundland dog hair, 2 ply.

MARGARET ZEPS • Brookings, Oregon
Crocheted Vest

The basic design for the vest comes from a sweater pattern in a magazine. It was a good pattern to adapt to handspun because the pieces were rectangular with little shaping. I especially liked the idea of the borders as an opportunity to use up small amounts of yarn from dye experiments.

In order to adapt the pattern to handspun yarn I did the following:

1. I made a diagram of the sweater. The dimensions were figured out both from instructions in the pattern (for example: crochet until piece measures 15" from beginning) and by translating number of stitches into inches from the gauge given.

2. I made a sampler of the yarn I wanted to use in order to see how many stitches per inch it would yield. This is the time to experiment with different hook sizes and different stitches to achieve the effect you want. By doing the sample you will know that if the yarn yields 5 stitches per inch and you need 18 inches, you must cast on 90 stitches.

3. I followed the actual directions of the pattern for shaping the pieces and assembling them, although this isn't necessary.

4. I only used the dimensions of the borders, but used my own ideas for color and stitch combinations.

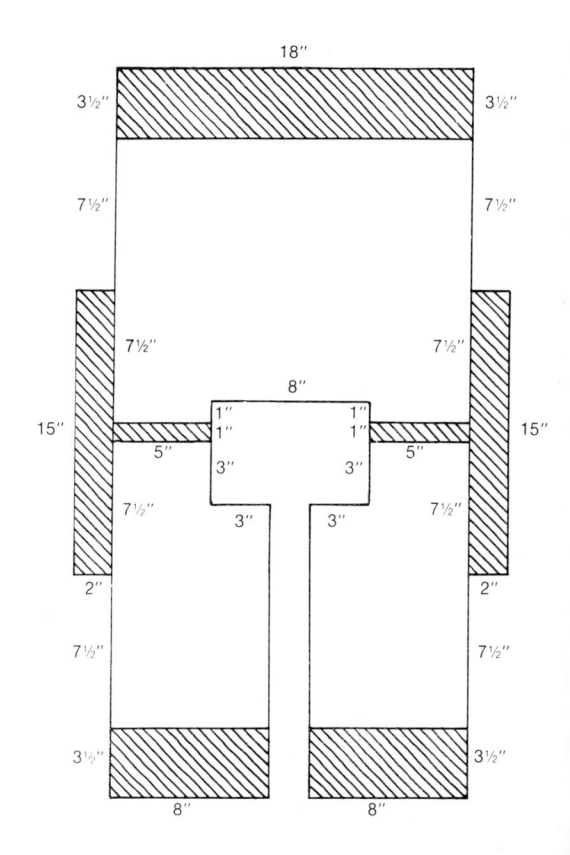

Photographs by Douglas Nidiffer.

Crocheted vest, grey Suffolk wool, naturally dyed Romney used in border.

Greentree Ranch Wools
163 N. Carter Lake Road
Loveland, Colorado 80537

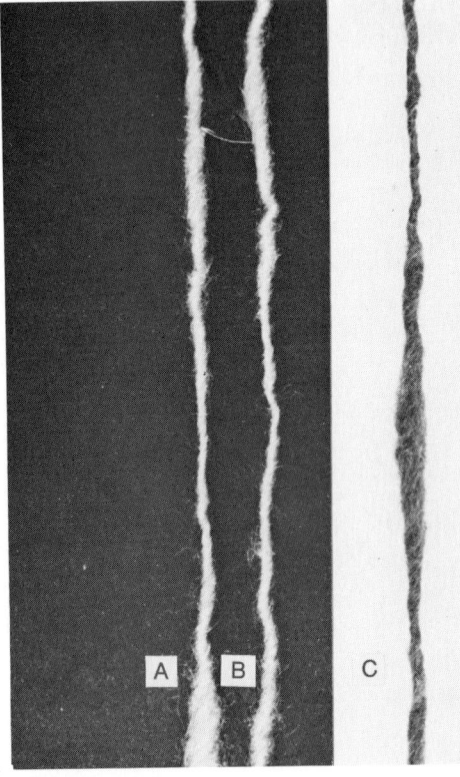

A, B Dyed Romney wool.
C Suffolk wool.

Detail of crocheted vest — border and front opening.

For the body of the vest, I decided to spin a medium weight singles yarn, approximating knitting worsted weight from some grey Suffolk fleece I had previously purchased from Greentree Ranch Wools, Loveland, Colorado. The fleece was teased and washed in cool water to remove the dirt, but not the lanolin. It was hand carded and spun on a wheel. The resulting yarn was a thick-and-thin yarn as is commonly produced by beginning spinners. This adds an interesting texture to the garment. After spinning, the yarn was washed in warm water and detergent, and weighted while drying to set the twist.

The green and chartreuse yarns were natural dyed the previous summer from plants in my yard. The wool was a white Romney fleece purchased locally. It was washed in cool water, dried, teased, hand carded, and spun on a wheel into a medium-weight singles yarn. It was scoured in hot water and detergent before dyeing. The recipes I used are based on Ida Grae's book, *Nature's Colors*. For both colors, the mordant was added directly to the dyebath rather than premordanting the wool.

Chartreuse:
1. Soak purple foxglove flowers *still on the stalks* overnight in cool water in a nonreacting pot (5 to 1 relation by weight of flower to wool or more).
2. The next day, bring to a simmer and simmer gently 30 minutes.
3. Strain flowers out of dyebath; cool slightly.
4. Dissolve correct amount of alum and cream of tartar for weight of wool being dyed in hot water. Add to dyebath and mix thoroughly.
5. Add scoured, presoaked wool.
6. Bring dyebath back to simmer, simmer wool in dyebath 1 hour.
7. Cool overnight in dyebath.
8. Rinse thoroughly and dry in shade.

Green:
1. Soak lavender dahlia flower heads (can be past prime bloom) in cool water overnight in a nonreacting pot (5 to 1 ratio by weight of flower to wool or more).
2. The next day, bring to simmer and simmer gently 30 minutes.
3. Strain flowers out of dyebath; cool slightly.
4. Dissolve correct amount of chrome and cream of tartar for weight of wool being dyed in hot water. Add to dyebath and mix thoroughly. Keep cover on pot from now on as chrome is affected by light.
5. Add scoured, presoaked wool.
6. Bring dyebath back to simmer, simmer wool in dyebath 1 hour.
7. Cool overnight in dyebath.
8. Rinse thoroughly and dry in shade.

Directions for vest pictured (size 34 to 36)

Amount of yarn used: Approximately 12 ounces grey and 2 ounces each chartreuse and green. This will vary according to yarn used.

Back and right front: (See diagram.) Chain correct number of stitches to measure 18". Do decorative border for 3½" (I used green and chartreuse yarn and a combination of rows of single, double, and popcorn stitches). Change to grey yarn, work even in half double crochet for 7½". Mark beginning and end of row for armholes. Continue to work even until armhole measures 6" from armhole marker ending at right armhole edge. Work across first 5" of back. Turn. Work even for 1". Do 2 rows of double crochet in decorative color (1"). Change back to grey yarn. Work even for 3" more ending at armhole edge. Work across the 5" and then chain enough extra stitches to measure 3". Work even for 11", do decorative border to match back (3½"). End off.

Left front: Start at left armhole edge of back and follow directions for right shoulder and front, reversing shaping.

Armhole caps: Mark armhole beginnings on front to correspond with back. Attach decorative yarn to wrong side at right front armhole marker, work single crochet stitches evenly spaced across armhole between markers, being careful not to draw work in. Do decorative border for 2". End off. Do same for left armhole.

Finishing: With decorative color, do a row of evenly spaced single crochet on wrong side of front openings and neck edge. Turn. On right side, do another row of single crochet forming button loops on right front edge where desired. Sew up side and underarm seams. Do row of single crochet around edges of armhole border. Use purchased buttons or crochet matching buttons.

Margaret modeling vest with assistant.

JOAN Z. ROUGH • **Danville, Vermont**
Poncho
Pullover Sweater
Child's Cardigan and Matching Cap
Baby Blanket

INTRODUCTION

The major source of inspiration for each of the following projects came from the colors and textures of my own handspun yarns. While I rarely spin that yarn with a specific project in mind, the articles made from it become statements of my own personal feelings and thinking with regards to how people can still relate as individuals to a modern and over-mechanized world. I wanted them to be primitive in nature, obviously hand-made, and to reflect the natural origins of the materials that went into them, both in texture and color.

In order to produce the kind of yarn that fulfills these expectations, I have learned to break many rules. It is true that breaking some rules has gotten me into a lot of trouble, but I have found that following them all leads to blandness, stagnation, and duplication of what everyone else is doing. In fact, rule-breaking can be creativity, and it is sometimes necessary for bringing about unique results. For instance, my fibres are not perfectly carded, and I have found that some overtwist in my spinning is often desirable. The resulting yarn gives a finished fabric a rich texture suitable for the most basic designs.

In weaving, I use only plain weaves, and in knitting, the simplest of stitches. Because of its texture, this yarn really does produce its own pattern, and attempts at anything too elaborate tend to become lost.

I get my fibres from several sources. For these four projects, the mohair came from my own Angora goats; the wool for the child's cardigan came from one of my own Romney sheep; and I got the gray wools for the pullover from a nearby sheep raiser.

As for the actual processing of my yarn, I will touch on it only briefly; my methods are fairly simple and straightforward. I process all my fibres in much the same manner: After discarding the unusable tags from the fleeces, I wash them, but I do not scour them in hot water; particularly with wool, I prefer to leave as undisturbed as possible the natural oils in the fleece, so that I can spin "in the grease." I then spread the wool out to dry on some old window screens. I treat mohair the same way, except I use warm water, which more easily softens the natural grease and relaxes the mohair fibres, easing further processing.

When the fleece is dry, I pick through it and begin teasing it in preparation for carding, discarding the pieces of hay and grass from our back pasture. I card it with a Curtis Fricke hand-carding machine, and I usually find that a single carding is sufficient. I prefer an uneven, lumpy yarn, and this is easier to spin when the fibres are not too perfectly aligned. For spinning the fibres, I use a Kircher wheel, which has a large orifice and permits me to spin a fairly bulky yarn. I give the yarn its thick and thin texture by drawing out the fibres unevenly, varying both the speed and the tension. This results in some over-spun and twisty texture, combined with some tufts of natural under-spun wool. After some experimenting, I found that I could produce a yarn every bit as strong as the machine-made variety, but it clearly has a unique, primitive, and natural individuality.

The next step is to wind the yarn into skeins and wash it again, this time in warm water and soap. If the yarn is to be dyed, it must be washed thoroughly in order to remove as much grease as possible. If not, I wash it only enough to set the twist and remove any remaining dirt, while letting some of the natural grease, with its high lanolin content and natural waterproofing properties, remain in the yarn.

Then comes dyeing for some of the yarns. I use a variety of dyeplants including marigolds, marsh marigolds, horsetails, goldenrod, mullein, sagebush, St. Johnswort, and onion skins. The specific plants used in dyeing the yarns for the baby blanket and the poncho are listed under those projects.

The dyeing is done in half-pound to one-pound batches; I use standard 18½ quart enameled canning pots. First the yarn is mordanted, using among others: alum, chrome, iron, and ammonia, in various combinations. Then the mordanted yarn is placed directly in the dye bath with the plant material. I prefer this "contact" method of dyeing because the colors seem to be stronger than when the dye bath is prepared ahead and the plants are removed.

What happens next is the most important step in my creative process. As I have said, it is the yarn itself which is the major source of my inspiration for a particular project. The visual characteristics of the yarn, its color and texture, as well as how it feels, actually dictate to me what it should be used for. For this reason, I like to have my yarn visible and within reach at all times while I'm working. I hang it up in every nook and cranny of my studio: on shelves, in baskets, and on the walls. I handle it and touch it frequently, and I can always see it while I'm working. Usually, the idea for a new project will come while I'm still in the middle of an old one, sitting at the loom and eyeing the properties of a particular skein of yarn across the room.

PONCHO

The poncho was the first of these four projects, and my first opportunity to weave with my own hand-spun mohair. It had been hanging in one section of my studio, where my attention was frequently drawn to it. It definitely seemed to call for something wearable. It was soft and lustrous, and it seemed to drape differently than the wool yarn hanging near it. I decided on a poncho, or as it is more traditionally known, a quesquemtle, to be woven on my large floor loom. My own rough-textured yarn is not particularly suited for a warp, so for this purpose I chose a relatively smooth, medium weight commercially prepared wool yarn. I dyed it in three batches: a light yellow, a gold, and a rust; and I threaded the loom for a plain weave, six ends per inch, in three sections, one for each color. For the weft, I chose four colors from the mohair: yellow, gold, rust, and medium gold. With this piece, as in much of my work, I preferred to improvise with the colors while I worked, rather than to do much pre-planning.

The subtle shading of the natural dyes can be trusted to have a nice effect in almost any combination, and I wanted to feel free to try out spontaneous ideas for color combination and variation. I simply wove the mohair onto the warp in a way which pleased me, and I decided on the areas of color and pattern as the weaving progressed. I wove two identical pieces, each measuring 20 by 40 inches, which when assembled would make a large size poncho. When they were removed from the loom, I knotted the warp to make a fringe and sewed the pieces together, the end of one butted to the side edge of the other, in the traditional way. I elected not to brush up the woven mohair to make it shaggy, as is often done. It would have destroyed the natural texture of my yarn, and I don't particularly care for the nose-tickling and shedding qualities of the brushed-up variety.

Materials Content:

Warp: Approx. 300 yards med. wt. wool yarn, "Donegal Homespun," from Tahki. Dyed as follows:

    Light yellow: Goldenrod, with alum mordant
    Light rust: Goldenrod, with chrome mordant
    Gold: Mullein, with alum and ammonia mordant

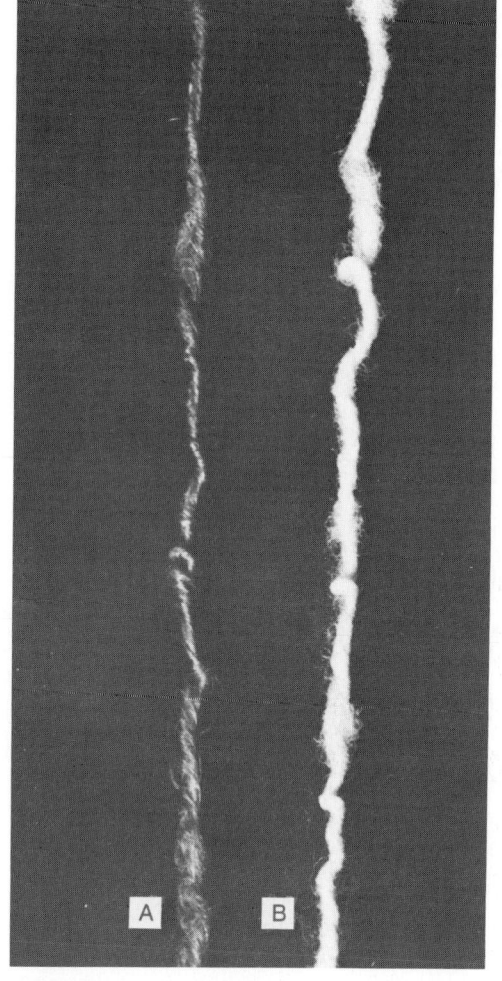

A Mohair.
B Wool, child's sweater.

Weft: Approx. 80 yards homespun mohair yarn, dyed as follows:
  Yellow: Marigolds, with alum mordant
  Gold: Horsetails, with chrome mordant
  Dark rust: St. Johnswort, with chrome and ammonia mordant
  Medium gold: Marsh marigolds, with chrome mordant

Photographs by Cougar Photography

Poncho, naturally dyed yarns. Commercial warp yarn, handspun mohair weft.

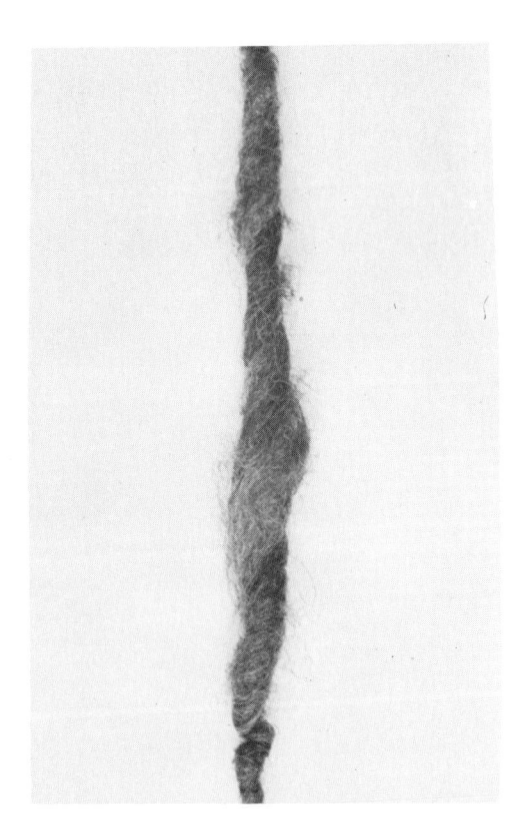

Sweater, one ply yarn, knitted in squares.

PULLOVER SWEATER

The gray pullover sweater represents the first time I used my own handspun yarns in knitting. Although the texture of the yarn was still the major factor, it and the other knitted patterns had some slightly different inspiration. I had been told by several friends and acquaintances that you simply can't knit with one-ply "lumpy" handspun yarn like mine. For a long time I had no inclination to take up the implicit challenge of such advice, since I was preoccupied with weaving. But eventually I grew more and more determined to give it a try. With needles in hand, and the "lumpiest" yarn I could find, I inevitably sat down to knit a sample. The resulting fabric had the beautiful rough texture which I admire and which has become my specialty; it was soft to the touch, and it was very heavy and strong. I used smaller needles than I might have otherwise chosen for that size yarn, and this resulted in a very tight knit. The garter stitch portion of the sample was reminiscent of a Persian lamb coat. I wouldn't choose to make socks from this material, but it seemed ideal for a "real" sweater, heavy and well suited to Vermont's upcoming winter.

For colors, I chose a blend of natural grays and black yarn that I had been eyeing on the wall of my studio for some time. Since the primary consideration this time was to be warmth, I would use all wool yarn anyway, and the darker colors do seem warmer. I quickly realized that knitting an adult-sized pullover in the conventional manner would be difficult, due to the

Texture — woman's sweater.

Woman's sweater, wool.

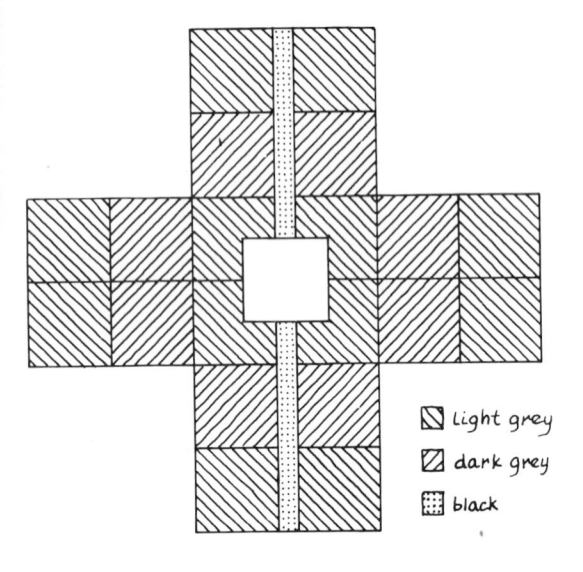

bulkiness of the yarn. So I decided to knit it in smaller blocks and strips that could be easily carried around, and that would not always be interfering with the needles. I made sixteen squares, and four others with an indentation in one corner to form the neckline, all from the gray yarn. Actually, I ran out of my original gray color, so I knitted some of the squares in a slightly darker shade and placed them in such a way as to give the finished sweater some very subtle color gradations. I also knitted two strips from black wool for the middle of the front and back of the sweater to give it some visual length and prevent the illusion of too much width and bulkiness. The diagram shows how the sweater was laid out.

In deciding on the exact size of the squares and strips, my own body measurements were the determining factor. When the knitting was completed, I first sewed together the small pieces, and then the sleeves and side seams. Several rows of single crochet served to round out the neck slightly and provide the finishing touches to the bottom and sleeves.

CHILD'S CARDIGAN AND MATCHING CAP

My next attempts at using my handspun yarn in knitting were for my 7-year-old daughter, Lisa, who declared that winter was coming and she too needed a new sweater. I chose some natural white wool yarn that I had spun from the fleece of one of my own Romney sheep, a favorite of Lisa's. It was of a lighter weight and not as bulky as the gray used in my own sweater. After knitting another sample, with a variety of stitches, I settled on a ribbed pattern, which seemed particularly well suited to my daughter's build and features. Again, I chose smaller needles to get the desired effect of a tightly knit fabric. This time, the sweater had to be a cardigan; my kids hate to pull sweaters on and off over their heads as often as they have to in this climate. I also decided to knit the sleeves somewhat longer than they needed to be, so that they could be folded up in a cuff-like manner. These longer sleeves would give some extra allowance for fast-growing arms, and they can also be pulled down over the hands on those chilly mornings when mittens have been forgotten. The sweater was knitted in the conventional manner: the back, two fronts, and two sleeves. And again, the specific proportions came directly from Lisa's own body measurements, and a pre-determined gauge of stitches-per-inch. I sewed the pieces together and finished off the sweater with a row of single crochet along the front edges and neckline.

The matching cap was knitted in the same "knit two purl two" rib pattern. This rib pattern knit stretches easily to fit most head sizes, and it is extremely warm and soft.

Texture — child's sweater.

Photographs by Cougar Photography Sweater and cap of Romney wool.

THE BABY BLANKET

The mohair baby blanket was the result of trying to come up with a unique but practical gift for Jesse, my about-to-be-born first nephew. Once again the yarn chose itself: that wonderful drape, and its soft, lustrous quality. Since I don't brush up the mohair, I felt it wouldn't be too fuzzy or shed, and it would make a safe, warm, and comfortable blanket for a new-born infant. I took my measurements from an old baby blanket and then took stock of my rapidly dwindling supplies of colored mohair yarn. I felt a patchwork affair of naturally dyed mohair would permit the wisest use of the few colors I had remaining. The more conventional pink or blue were out of the question, as I didn't have them, and he wasn't born yet so I didn't know which. Besides, I am not overly fond of the "sameness" of "baby colors"; I saw no reason not to instill in my new nephew a sense of his own uniqueness and a love for the colors of the natural world.

Mon Tricot Knitting and Crochet Dictionary (provided helpful tips on knitting the 90° angles of the border strip).

For yarn samples, see poncho.

I chose a muted green, a rust, a gold, and a yellowish green. Once I had determined the correct size for each square, I knitted thirty of them in the various colors. Since I wanted the blanket to look and feel the same on both sides, I used a garter stitch. I laid them out in a variety of pleasing patterns before I settled on the one I liked best. Then I sewed them together and added a separately knitted border strip. A row of single crochet around the outside edge was the finishing touch.

Dyeing information:

Light rust:	Goldenrod with chrome mordant
Yellowish green:	Goldenrod with alum mordant
Gold:	Onion skins with chrome mordant
Muted green:	Sagebush with chrome and iron mordant

Baby blanket, knitted in squares, border continuous strip, handspun mohair, natural dyes.

CONCLUSION

After I had completed each of these four projects, the final finishing steps were all similar. They were carefully washed one last time, and blocked; I used cool water and a mild soap. I wrapped them in a towel to absorb excess moisture, and then laid them out flat to dry. A light steam treatment with my iron was the final touch.

The blanket, the sweaters, and the poncho are all unique, one-of-a-kind items. They are not the usual fare to be found in the neighborhood department store. They are also all practical items. They represent my attempt to express the personal feeling that maybe we can do a bit more for ourselves, and maybe we can stay a bit closer to the natural world than our civilized world might lead us to believe.

BUCKY KING • Sheridan, Wyoming

Tapestry Bags

All the wool in these bags is from my own sheep or the sheep of our neighbors. I own crossbreed Columbian, Panamas (which I feel are the best) and crossbreed Targees. Since I own my own sheep I am able to wash them in the morning before I shear them in the evening. Then I spin the wool in the grease. With white fleece I intend to dye with natural dyes. I wash the whole fleece first unless it is one of my own. If my own, I spin in the grease and then scour the skeins thoroughly before dyeing them.

For these bags I used handspun 2 ply, double-spun, for warp set at 4 to 5 epi. All the yarn was spun on my Ashford wheel with large orifice. The wool was hand carded.

Most of the yarns were used in their natural colors. However, I did use some natural dyes; the gold and tan are from goldenrod, using a chrome mordant.

The design was worked from a tiny sketch. I rarely make cartoons unless lettering is needed.

JANET HETZLER • Signal Mountain, Tennessee

Knit Circular Mohair Shawl

Fiber: The fiber was clean, white mohair roving from Clemes & Clemes Spinning Wheels, 650 San Pablo Ave., Pinole, CA 94564.

Spinning: The mohair was spun on a flax wheel into a single-ply medium fine yarn. No carding or other preparation was necessary. I pulled off a staple length and spun it from the middle of the piece. It required a certain amount of concentration while spinning because it was so clean and silky. After knitting with it, it seems like I should have washed or wet it to set the twist better, since it was a little unruly at times.

Design: The idea for the shawl evolved from three separate things: 1) my love of knitted shawls, blankets, and afghans; 2) my fascination with knitting circles and squares; 3) the fact that I had bought and spun only one pound of the mohair.

My problem was to make something pretty and useful while making the most efficient use of my one pound of yarn. I decided to knit a circular shawl, and started with size 10 double-pointed needles, and a gauge of 3 to 3½ sts per inch. I used the large needles because I knew I was looking for an open, lacy pattern. Gauge is not terribly important in unfitted, knitted items like shawls or afghans, unless you're aiming for a

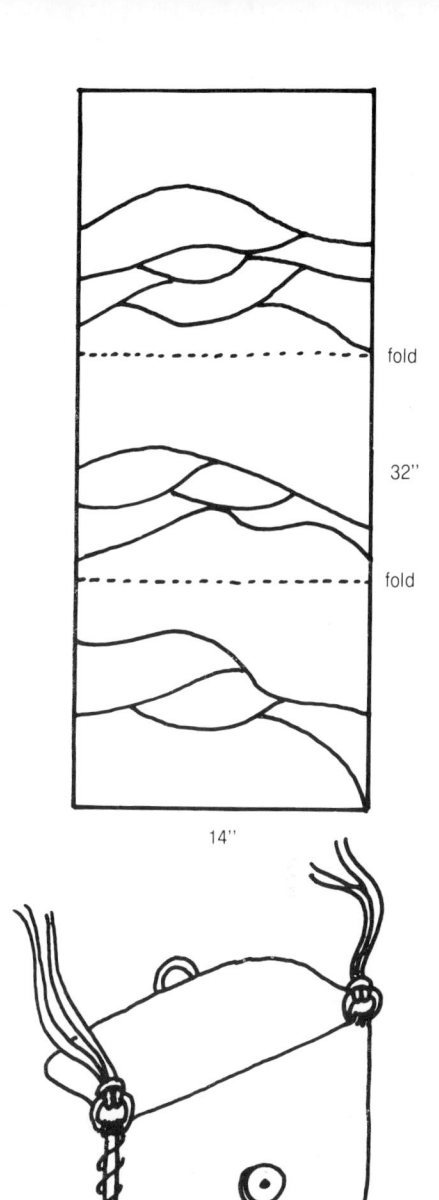

Lining — heavy weight interfacing 13" x 31". Lining fabric machine stitched to inside over interfacing.

Tapestry bags shown in color; see front pages.

Knitter's Almanac
Elizabeth Zimmerman
(A required book for anyone who loves to knit. There are detailed instructions for circular and square knitting.)

A New Look at Knitting
Elyse and Mike Sommers
(good — lots of ideas)

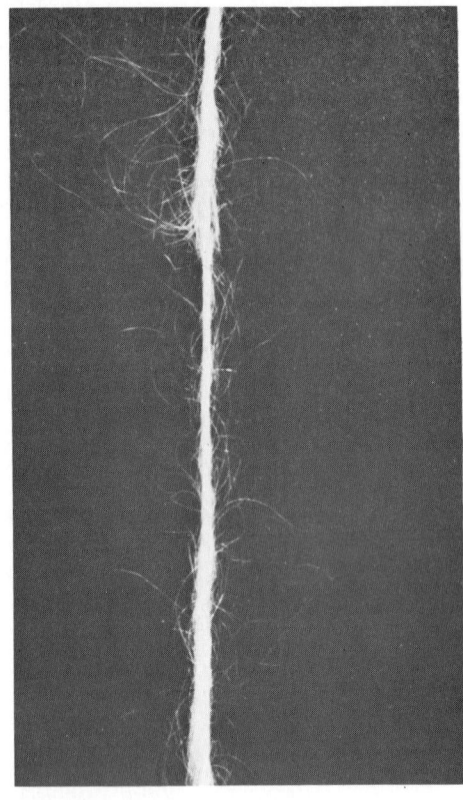

Mohair.

specific size. (I included my gauge only to give an idea of what I was working with.) I have found that a circle or square knitted from the center out works beautifully with a limited or unknown amount of yarn because you can work with the basic shape until you run out of yarn, while having the freedom to work in any knitting pattern as you go. The end product can always be used as a shawl, lap robe, or baby blanket.

The basic idea involved in knitting a circle or square is to start with a small number of stitches (6 to 12) equally divided on three or four double-pointed needles, and knit in rounds, shaping the knitting as you go by increasing at regular intervals. A circle is shaped by doubling the number of stitches, at first fairly often, and then at increasingly larger intervals in order to keep the knitting flat, while a square is shaped by increasing one stitch on either side of four equidistant stitches every other row. When I get too many stitches to knit comfortably on the double-pointed needles, I switch to a circular needle.

You can begin to work in any pattern you like, whether traditional or improvised, when you have enough stitches to accommodate, in a circle, three repeats evenly spaced, and in a square, four repeats, one to a side. As your knitting gets larger, you can add more repeats.

For this shawl, I used a random pattern of yarnovers followed by a knit-2-together decrease to keep the number of stitches constant. I varied the number of overs in the yarnovers to get different size holes, and also varied the number of stitches between the yarnovers to change the placement of the lacy holes. I followed each pattern row by a knit row. One really important thing to remember in this type of knitting is that you always have the same side facing you, but traditional patterns are written for knitting that is turned after each row. This means that in circular knitting you have to knit the purls, and purl the knit stitches on every other row.

One problem with trying to use all the yarn you have by knitting from the center out is knowing when to stop so as to leave yourself enough yarn for casting off. I have not found a really satisfactory way of dealing with this other than to know the yardage of your skeins and to keep track of how many rows each skein knits up. I can guess from this how many yards to leave for finishing. When I had about three ounces of yarn left, I began finishing up by knitting six rounds of plain knitting. The plain knitting sort of ruffled up a little, making a nice edge for a lacy shawl.

Since lace patterns spread a lot when you take them off the needle, before casting off I slipped the stitches onto a piece of string and blocked the shawl drastically by dampening it and pinning it out until completely dry. Then I put the stitches back on the needle and cast off. If I had cast off first, the castoff edge might very well have been too tight to give with the spread. After blocking, the finished size was sixty inches in diameter,

Photographs by T. Fred

Circular shawl by Janet Hetzler — knitted from center out, handspun mohair singles.

and out of the pound of yarn, I had used fourteen to fifteen ounces.

The possibilities for circles and squares are endless. When someone gave me a bag of tiny skeins of vegetable-dyed yarn, I knitted them into small squares and needle-wove them together into a beautiful multicolored baby blanket. You could use the technique for things like pillows or placemats, or to use up odds and ends of different yarns. It's also very portable work, and therefore easy to carry along for those of us who always love to have a project with us.

Detail of shawl. Center of pattern is in the upper left hand corner of photo.

KRISTA D'VINCENT • Vista, California
Rainbow Runner
Inlay Raw Fleece Hangings
Afghan
Swedish Rosepath Rug
Poncho

I live on a sunny hillside in Vista. We have ¾ of an acre with fruit trees, flowers, and a vegetable garden which grows year round in our mild weather.

We have a small flock of 15 hens, a turkey, a nanny goat; three sheep and two angora goats that I get plenty of wool and mohair from.

Our cottage has only one room and a built-in loft. We heat with a wood stove and cook a lot of what we grow in the garden.

I do all my spinning outside in the garden near the animals, using a New Zealand Ashford wheel with a bulk head so that I can get thicker yarn and more yardage to each skein. I generally work with bulky yarns. Recently I acquired a carding machine which has greatly speeded up the process.

Plant dyes are easy to find in the surrounding fields and in my garden. I generally gather up dye stuff and dye the same day rather than drying and storing it.

Shearing time is once a year for the sheep, twice a year for the angora goats. I use blade shears, and do it myself. I still have to send away to England, New Zealand, and various parts of the U.S. for extra fleece. I like to use a variety of different hairs and fleeces in my work.

Most of my weaving is done on a 30" folding Pendleton loom.

Because of our minimal space I hang my skeins of wool from high dowels or ball the yarn and fill up baskets until I'm ready to use it. The yarn gives a nice warm feeling to the room.

RAINBOW RUNNER

I first got the idea for this rug when I was given the use of a loom that was already threaded with a very strong wool rug warp set at 5 epi in a basket weave. I had a few weeks to think about what to make with this lovely gift. It was an open canvas.

It was springtime, everything was blooming, and as I sat out in the garden with my spinning wheel, I began to plan a rug that would reflect the colors of spring. Inspired by Ida Grae's book, "Nature's Colors" I would spin and dye two skeins a day until I had enough yarn to begin weaving.

The bulk of the yarn used in this piece came from an overweight Suffolk sheep which belonged to a friend. The wool dyed well and spun easily from the locks into a thick spongy yarn. The rest of the yarn came from odds and ends of handspun wool that I had accumulated through years of experiments with vegetable dyeing.

The rug has about 75 different colors in it, and only a few of the dyestuffs were purchased. The rest were gathered in the garden and the fields. I used leaves and bark from trees; flowers,

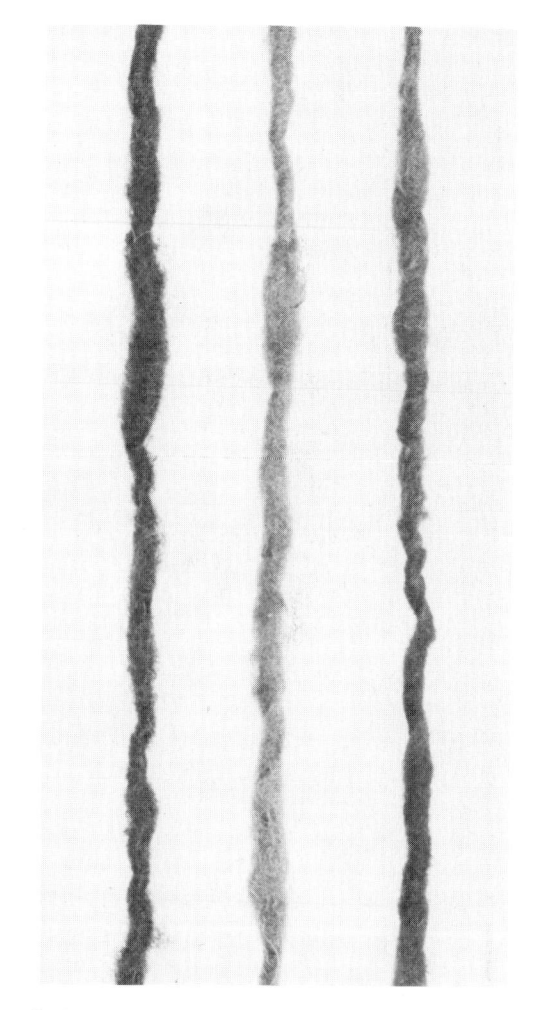

Suffolk wool.

Rainbow runner shown in color; see front pages.

leaves, and stems from plants; lichens; roots; and bugs.

Each day I started a new dyepot and put in the two skeins I had spun the day before. My dyeing system is simple. I put chopped-up vegetable matter, mordants, and wet yarn all together in the same dyepot and heat slowly for up to several hours at a temperature just below a simmer, stirring occasionally. The yarn stays overnight in the dyepot, cooling. In the morning I rinse out the yarn well in cold water and dry it in the shade.

When I had all my skeins I arranged them in rainbow fashion and wove short stripes blending this odd array of color as best I could.

I had no idea how long the warp was, but I knew that small stripes would help to keep the colors from being used up too soon. When I finished after 10½ feet I had colors left over.

The rug was entered in the 1977 Southern California Expo at Del Mar in the Home Arts and won first place and a special award.

INLAY RAW FLEECE HANGINGS & RUG

This technique is an excellent way to use up extra fleece. I can easily use up half a fleece in a 2½ by 3 foot weaving. I gradually developed my methods, at first because I had a lot of extra fleece that I didn't have time to work with, and then becoming fascinated by the possibilities. Ideas grew into more ideas as I sat at the loom working.

All three of these pieces were woven in essentially the same way. I thread the loom in a tabby weave at 4 epi using a commercial rug wool for the warp. Then I start laying in the barely roved dirty greasy fleece. Five or six rows of rug wool are woven in between each row of inlay. I use a plain tabby weave usually and pack it in very tightly if I am making a rug. Wall hangings don't need to be worked as tightly. Usually, the fleece is not even carded. I tease it a bit, sort it a little and pick out the obvious thorns and stickers. Long staple fiber seems to work the best although I do throw in short staple for more bulk at times.

I've experimented and found many different ways to do inlay. One method is to pull a finger full of inlayed fleece slightly up between the warp threads. This makes a sort of "pocking" effect. (See figure 1).

In figure 2 I've taken mohair, llama, alpaca, and New Zealand wool and blended them into a natural color pattern. This hanging is very soft and wonderful to feel. It measures 28" by 32".

In figure 3 I've taken all long karakul fleece in the natural colors and inlayed by overlapping half a tuft of fleece over the preceding tuft of fleece and left the other half of the tuft hanging out in places. The rest of the fleece is simply laid in like unspun roving and beaten down. This wall hanging measures 56" by 30".

Photograph by Les Rodrigues.

Detail of inlay raw fleece hanging.

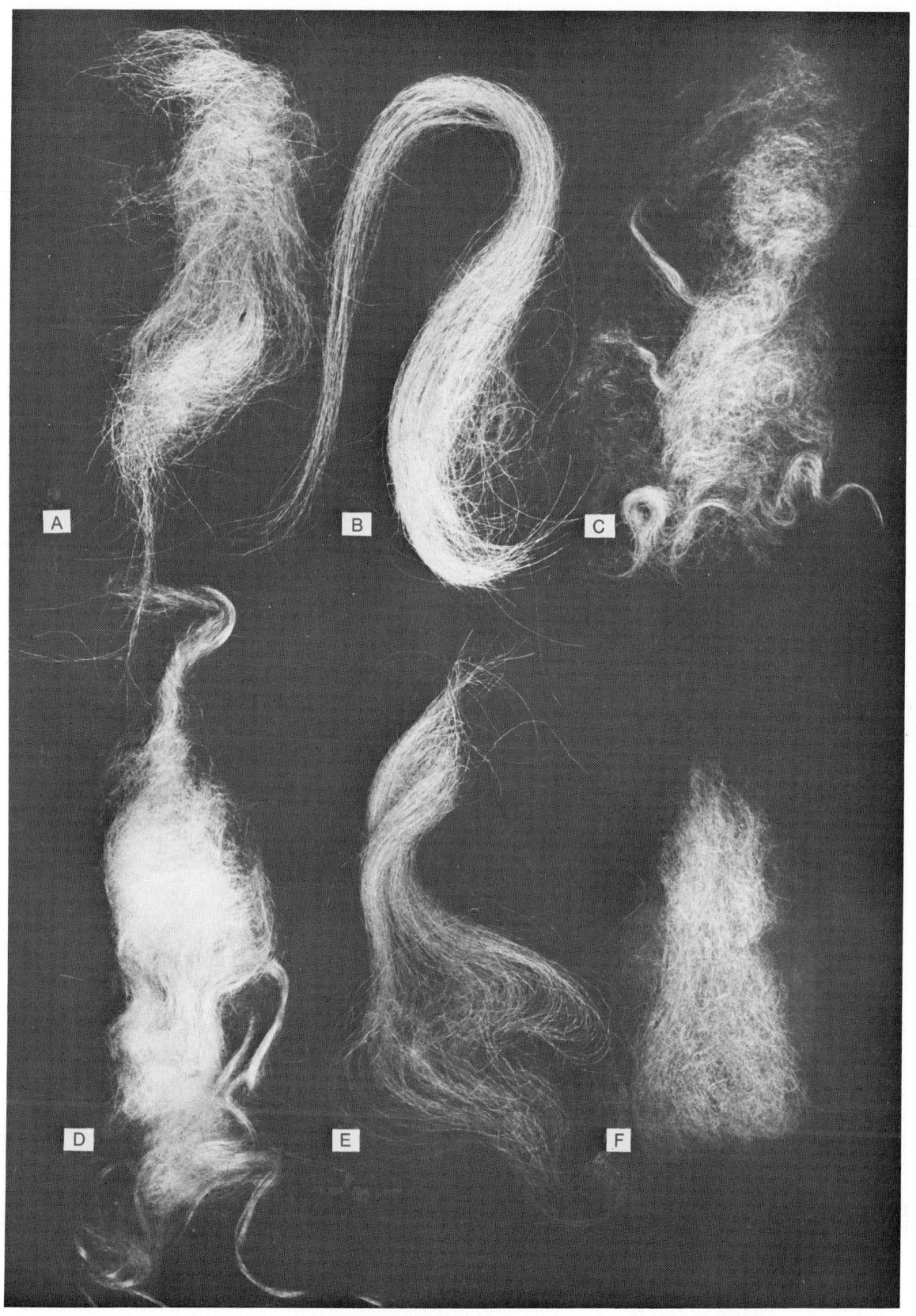

A Yearling karakul.
B Two year old karakul ram.
C Romney.
D Mohair.
E Karakul yearling ram.
F Llama.

When I finish weaving an inlay piece it is cut off the loom, the ends are tied in a lark head knotting and then it is thrown into a tub of very hot water. Next it is rinsed, then washed in a liquid detergent (actually scrubbed a bit). After being washed, I continue on through the hot and cold phases of felting. When it has been rinsed for the final time it is hung out to dry over a wooden bar and then I've got a fine felted rug or hanging (or anything else I choose to call it).

Karakul wool and mohair both have wonderful felting qualities and work out beautifully, in this type of work. A final advantage is that it is a much quicker way to get a finished piece than spinning all the yarn and then doing a "regular" weaving.

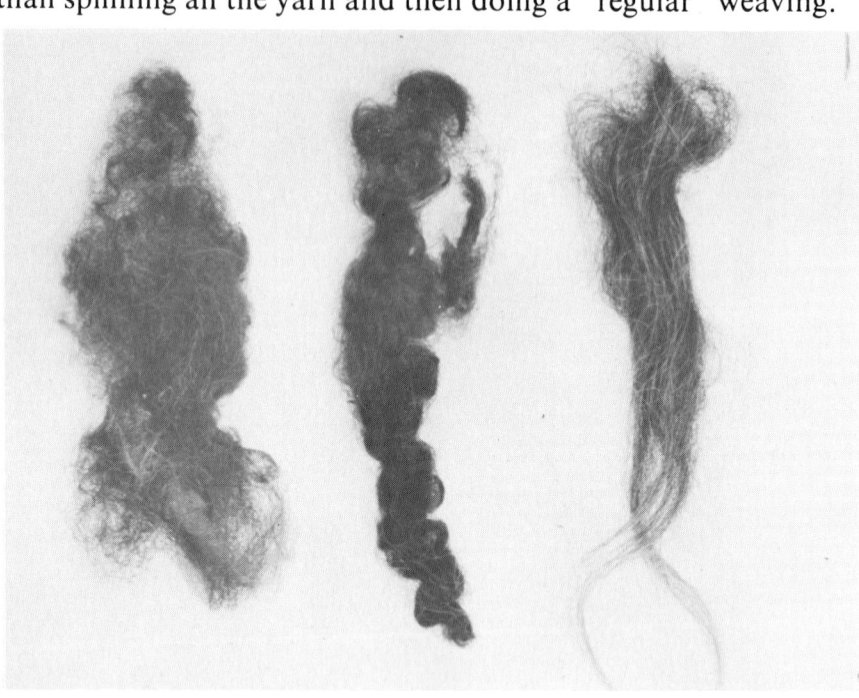

Alpaca.   Romney.   Karakul ewe.

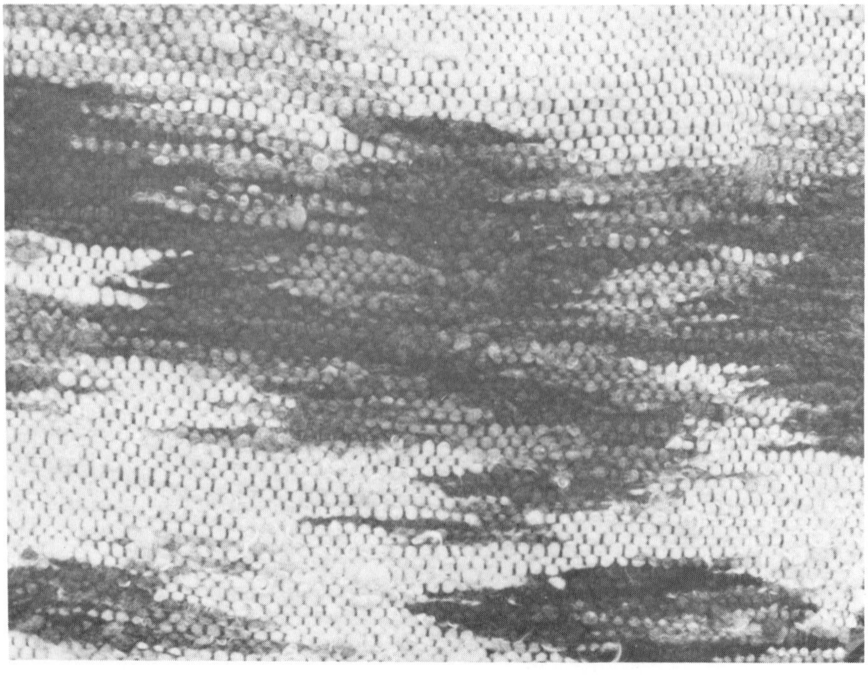

Swedish Rosepath rug, all handspun yarns. (See page 42)

Photograph by Les Rodrigues.

Figure 2. Mohair, llama, alpaca, New Zealand wool in a natural color pattern.

Figure 1. Inlay raw fleece rug with "pocking."

Figure 3. Raw fleece hanging: karakul in the natural colors.

Photograph by Les Rodrigues.

AFGHAN 3' BY 5'

Weaving this afghan was an interesting experience. I started with New Zealand Romney wool in various shades of browns and grays and also white. The wool was very nice, oily, clean, rather long staple, and with a tendency to hold together as locks. It was easy to spin without carding (easier, actually, than carding it first would have been). The method I use for spinning uncarded wool is fairly simple. Take a lock of wool and tease a little. Hold the fibers at the tip to join onto the yarn and begin

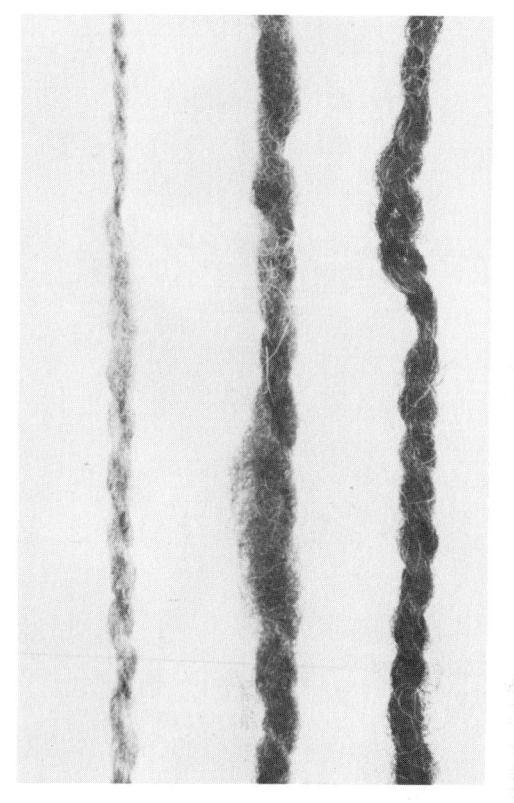

Warp yarns.

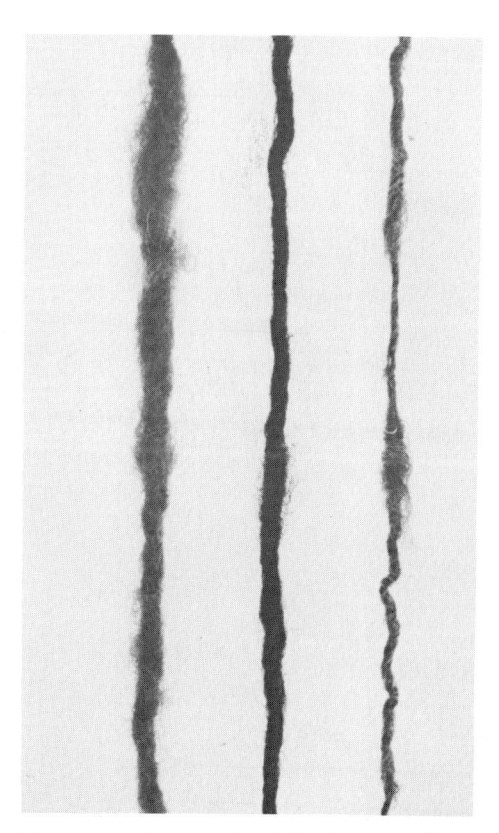

Weft yarns, New Zealand Romney, singles.

Photograph by Les Rodrigues. Krista D'Vincent wrapped in her totally handspun afghan.

A,B Karakul, weft.
C Warp, karakul.
D Warp, New Zealand Romney.

A Handweaver's Pattern Book
Marguerite P. Davison

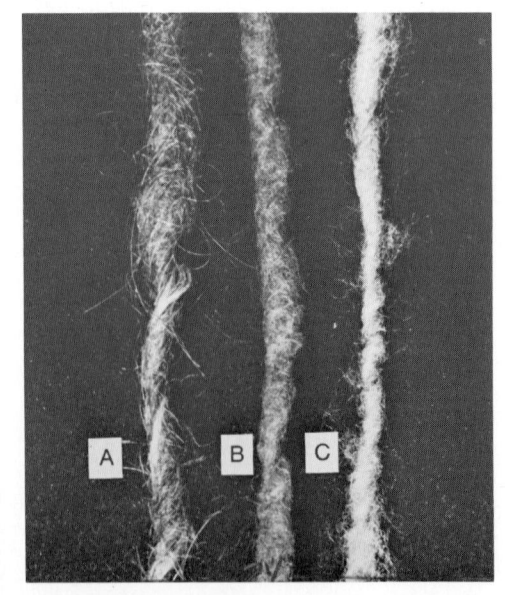

A Camel hair, weft.
B,C Romney wool, weft.

spinning. Tease continually with one hand while the other hand controls the twist.

I plyed the yarns for the warp and sett them at six ends per inch on an 18" 4 harness "Structo" table loom. The sett was actually 12 epi as I was weaving it double width. The warp was about 8½' long. Takeup was about 1½'. Fringes took up another 2'. The weft yarns were all singles.

I never should have loaded so much wool onto such a small loom. The warp was too bulky and thick for 6 ends per inch let alone 12 ends per inch through a 6 dent reed! I literally wrecked my loom by struggling with the warp trying to roll it on the back beam and then when I was weaving, forward onto the breast beam. In fact the yarn was so packed on the loom I had to literally not weave several 2, 3, and 4 inch spaces which I put in later with a needle when the afghan was off the loom. It was barely possible to get a shed, because the levers on the loom were so difficult to pull up. The warp threads stuck to each other rather badly. I was very lucky that the afghan turned out well.

It was, however, an extremely valuable learning experience for a self-taught weaver.

SWEDISH ROSEPATH RUG 19" BY 30"

When I first started spinning I didn't weave. I would spin yards of lovely yarn, ply it, and wonder what to make. So I decided to just weave up what I'd spun. This led to weaving with handspun warp.

This rug was one of three experimental weavings done on a handspun warp. I used plyed New Zealand Romney and plyed karakul from my own sheep. The arrangement of the rosepath in this weaving is my own idea, but the threading is from *A Handweaver's Pattern Book*. It is made entirely from my own handspun yarns.

I dyed some of the Romney with seasonal desert white forget-me-not roots (blue from alum mordant), onion skins (orange, again with alum), and Desert Pinion (yellow, no mordant). I also used undyed karakul in the warp. The weft is Romney, karakul, and camel hair.

The loom was threaded at 6 epi. I have found that handspun warp is easy to work with if you are careful to get all the same type of fleece. Otherwise tension can be a little bit of a problem. I also ply my handspun before using it for warp.

It is a wonderful feeling to do everything yourself, from raising the animals, spinning and dyeing the yarn, to weaving the cloth.

PONCHO

Weaving is a process of creating problems and then solving them.

My Pendleton loom was new at the time and it had 5 feet of beautiful "Cum" warp on it set in a birdseye pattern at 4 epi. The inspiration for the poncho came from the beautiful warp on my new loom. The yarn was fawn golden brown and looked pretty with my natural handspun yarn.

The handspun yarns are from Peruvian alpaca, Asian camel down, mohair from my own goats, and New Zealand wool. All of these yarns were odds and ends that I had hanging around my studio. I chose yarns of different weights and textures to add interest. I also used "Indecita" 100% alpaca yarn by Michell & CIA, S.A. in the weft. This made the poncho softer and lighter weight. All of the yarns were washed before weaving. Shrinkage on the finished garment was minimal, both because the yarns were prewashed, and because alpaca does not shrink very much.

During the weaving I experimented with variations on the threading and played around with the possibilities of the yarns.

The tapestry of the swallow in the center front was woven in on the loom just before the split for the neck.

The poncho wears well and is very warm.

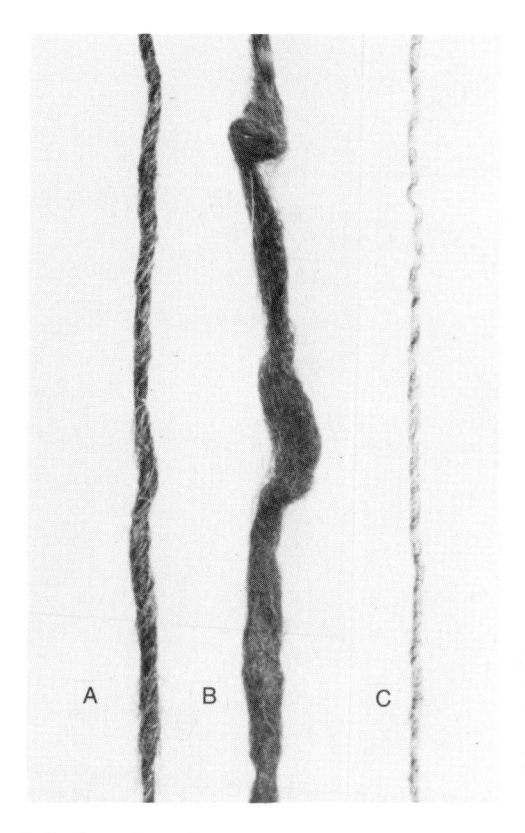

A, B Peruvian alpaca.
C Wool.

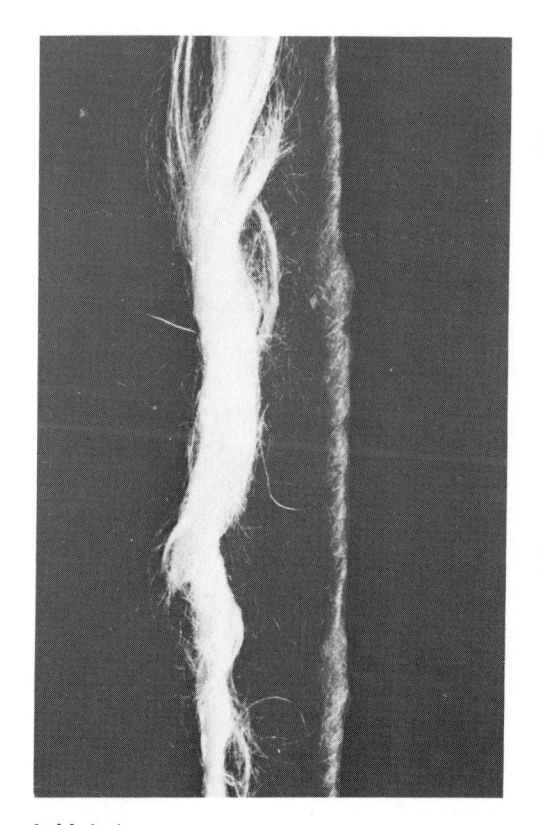

A Mohair.
B Asian camel down.

Photograph by Les Rodrigues.

Handspun alpaca, camel down, mohair, New Zealand wool. Commercial warp.

The Wool Factory
1246 N. Hwy. 101
Leucadia, CA 92024

The Black Sheep
1010 First Street
The Old Market
Encinitas, CA 92024

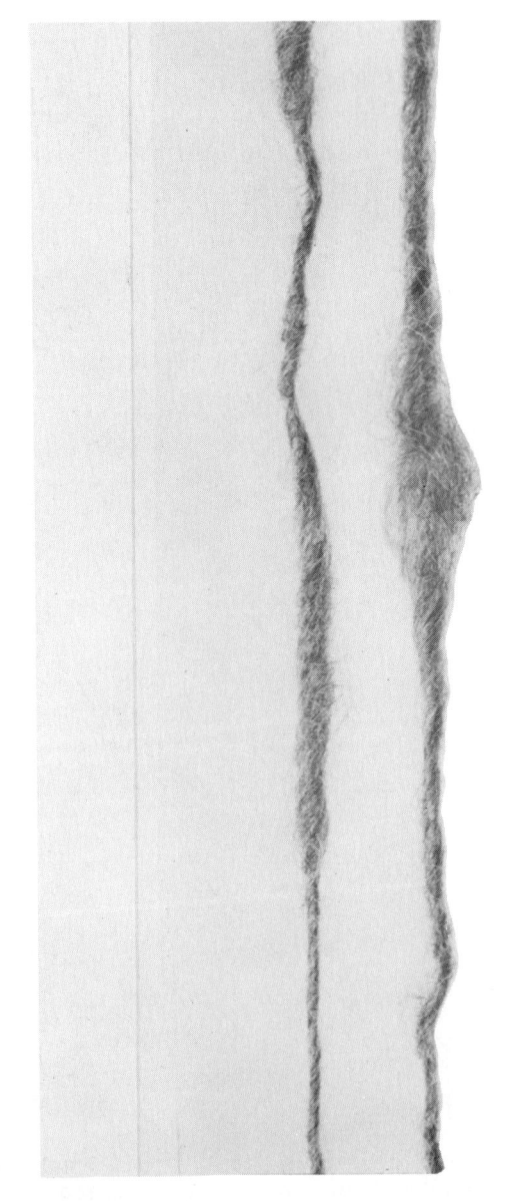

Romney

JULIANNE EATON • Encinitas, California
Hooded Jacket

I found a beautiful New Zealand Romney silver grey fleece in a small Encinitas shop, the Wool Factory. The fleece was very clean. It had a beautiful sheen and the tips had a curl. It was so nice that it required very little teasing before spinning. I had no garment planned when I purchased the fleece.

I spin on a Johansen wheel. It is a saxony type, heavy oak wheel with a double drive band. While I was spinning I decided to make a jacket. In designing the pattern I decided on the hood idea in the Burhenoose pattern from *"Weaving You Can Wear"* by Jean Wilson and Jan Burhen. I wanted sleeves on the jacket, so with help from some weaver friends at The Black Sheep in Encinitas, we developed a paper pattern to determine the dimensions. We settled on ¾ length sleeves to eliminate a 20" width at the wrist.

The fleece was spun in the grease and then washed in soap and water. The end result was a beautiful shiny silver. The warp I chose was a commercial 2 ply alpaca-llama mix which I used in three colors, black, grey, and white. I wanted the jacket to have black and white warp stripes. I wove it 36 inches wide on a 4 harness floor loom. It was sett at 6 ends per inch and woven in a tabby weave. To add a finishing touch when the jacket was completed I sewed an eleven strand braid of warp and weft yarns to the sleeves and midriff.

Detail of Juli's coat, showing finishing.

Photograph by Les Rodrigues.

Julianne's coat. Handspun New Zealand Romney combined with a 2 ply alpaca-llama yarn (commercial).

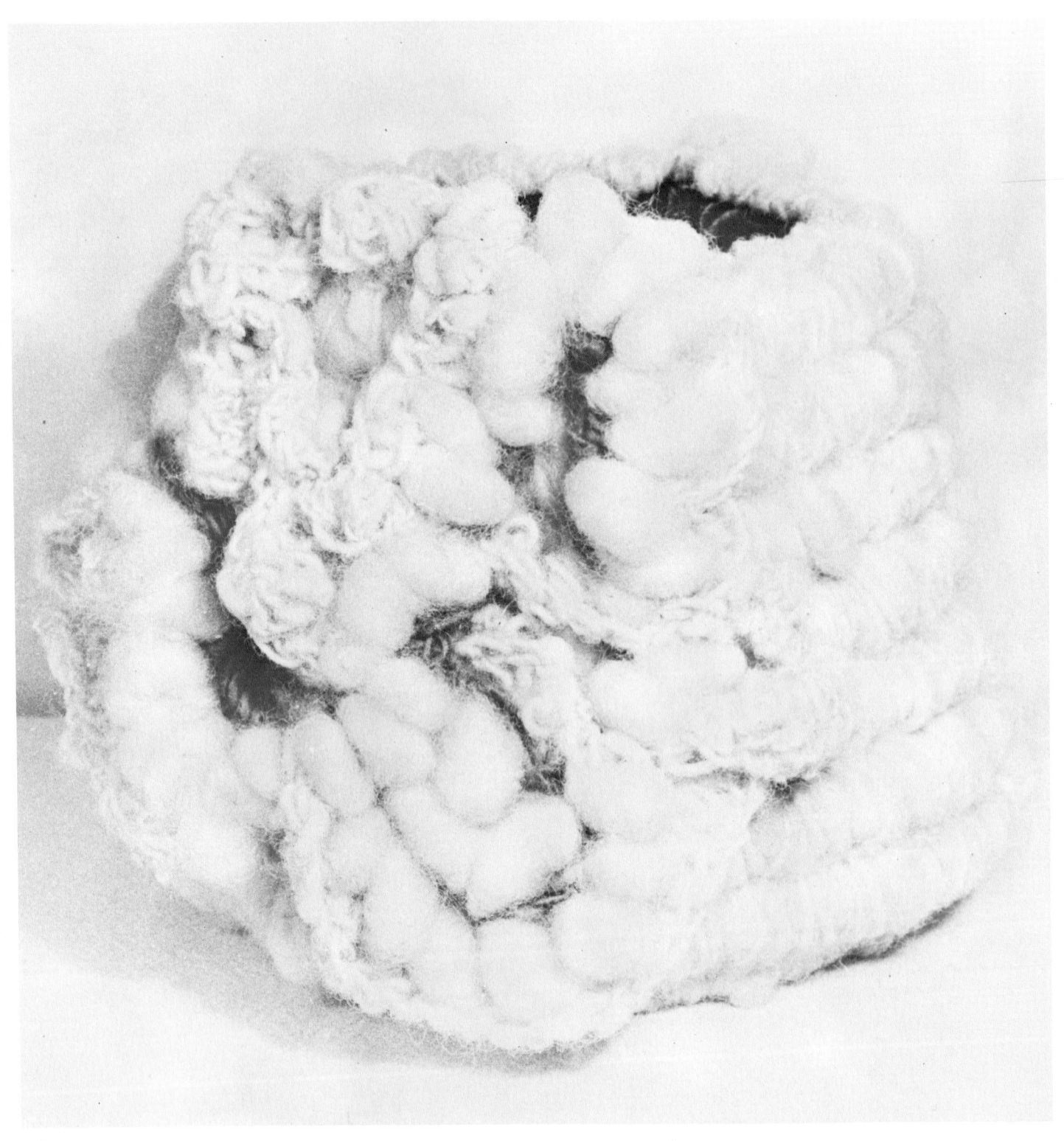

Light basket.

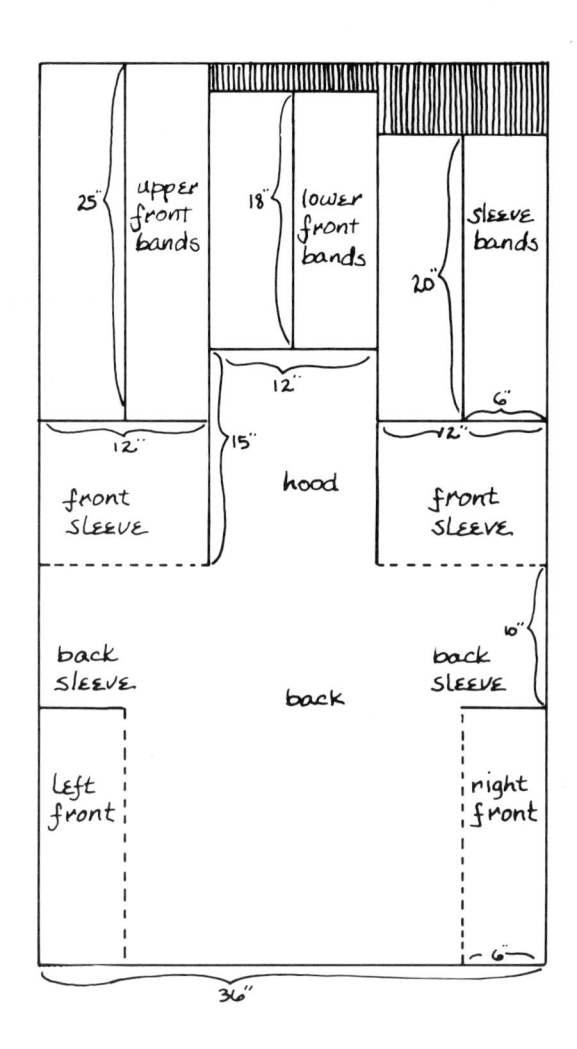

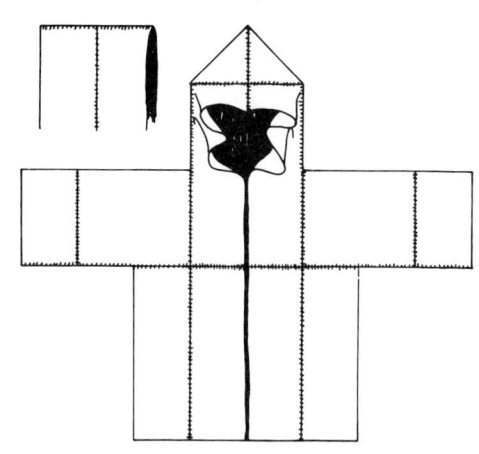

NANCY PIATKOWSKI • Kenmore, New York
Crocheted Baskets
Bags of Handspun Karakul

Front band sections may be woven as a continuous piece omitting seam on front band at midriff. Add 18" lower front band to 25" upper front band in pattern diagram. Adjust warp yardage. Leftover warp might be used to make a matching purse or a small pillow.

To sew: I used a sewing machine. Always cut between double rows of zig-zag stitching. Fold top of hood section in half and sew. Sew upper front band sections together. Match hood seam to upper band seam. Sew upper front band section down front of hood and upper body of jacket to midriff. Sew sleeve additions on. Add lower front band sections to front of coat and sew. Fold sides in and sleeves down. Sew underarm and midriff seams.

Use of separate shuttles recommended to eliminate raveling.

CROCHETED BASKETS

The original ideas for the baskets pictured came from *New Design in Crochet* by Clinton MacKenzie. I took his basic techniques of increase and decrease, worked with them until I felt I had control and then took off. I find I like simple shapes with the emphasis on the ornamentation. Much of my inspiration comes from primitive baskets and clay objects of all ages. The ornamentation often reflects American Indian influence.

DARK BASKET
"Handspun and Greek" 4"h x 6"d

The yarns used in the basket were a black handspun wool and a commercial spun Greek goat hair used together as a double strand in the body of the basket.

The handspun was done from a natural black wool roving. It was spun on the Penguin Quill. The goat hair was added for

Wool.

Detail of light basket.

Wool crocheted over core of "Woolspinneri." Ornamentation partly with naturally dyed wool.

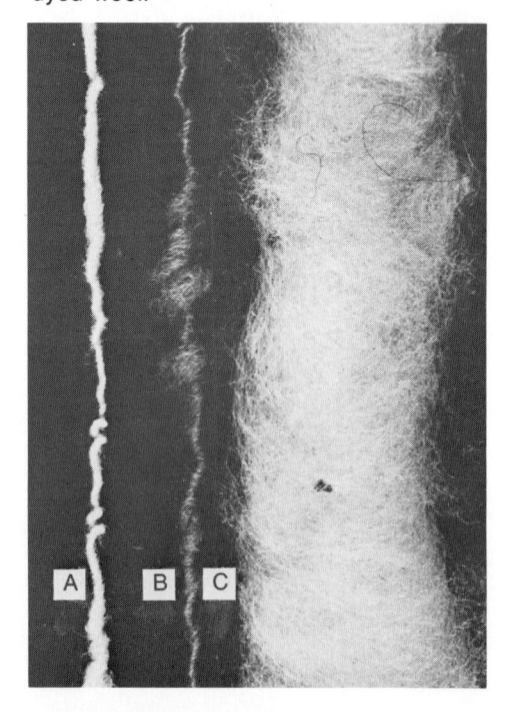

A Hampshire.
B Hampshire, dyed with carrot tops.
C Core — "Woolspinneri" (Green Tree Ranch Wools) not handspun.

Handspun wool crocheted together with Greek goat hair. 4 x 6 inches.

strength and contrast as the wool alone was too soft to support the shaping of the basket (no armature was used). I used an aluminum crochet hook, size J. The bottom was worked with single crochet until the correct size was obtained. The sides were worked with no increases until as high as desired. I find it takes two or three rows of working with no increase until a definite side takes shape. Two rows of handspun were pulled into loops through the spaces of the crochet. Shell slices were sewn around the top and Lady Amherst pheasant feathers were glued between the shells. (I use Velvrette by SOBO to fasten the feathers.) It was lined with dark brown velvet.

LIGHT BASKET

"Winter's Other Name" 5"h x 6"d at base, 4"d at top

The technique used in this basket was different from the one in the dark basket. I used handspun white wool and crocheted over a core of Woolspinneri Alpen Wool. The shaping was done as in the dark basket but because of the softness of the core a much more irregular shape was obtained. I found that when the piece was done I liked the inside texture better so I turned it inside out. The ornamentation was crocheted directly to the basket. Random single crochet stitches were hooked into the base. Then I worked over this area with more crochet using single, double and triple stitches — ruffling and gathering as I felt. I used a soft natural dyed green handspun to add detail inside the white areas. Puffs of wool roving were pulled through the crocheting for added detail. (The idea being to suggest the green of spring hidden in the snow of winter.) The basket was lined in a green velvet that matched the green wool.

BAGS OF HANDSPUN KARAKUL

The yarn used for the body of the bags was a single ply, natural gray/black karakul. It was spun on the Toika flyer wheel after washing and teasing. Because of the staple length (6" to 8"), carding was impossible. The result was a very hairy, tweedy yarn. It was skeined, washed again and dried under tension. (I've been using a button display rack from a fabric store to dry yarn — the little hooks are far enough apart to hold any size skein.)

The yarn used in the inlay was a Penguin Quill spun bulky wool. The fleece used (breed unknown) was a mix of light/dark gray to brown. It was washed and rough carded. Part had felted slightly in the washing so a rough texture was easily obtained. The twist was not set.

The warp was a fine dark brown commercial single ply yarn used double and sett at 10 epi.

The bags developed on the loom. I knew I wanted something rough and primitive but that was all. The yarns were selected because of the contrast in texture (one was rough and hairy, the other soft and nubby). The dangles were put together after the bags were woven. The beads, complimenting the color of the yarn, looked old and primitive. The tin cones were selected because of the noise they make when the bags are worn as were the sea urchin spines.

The backs were woven in tabby. The loops on Bag #1 were done using the slip knot on p. 48 of *Pile Weaves* by Jean Wilson. For the inlay on either side of the dangle on Bag #1, two butterflies were used. For the area across the top, rows of

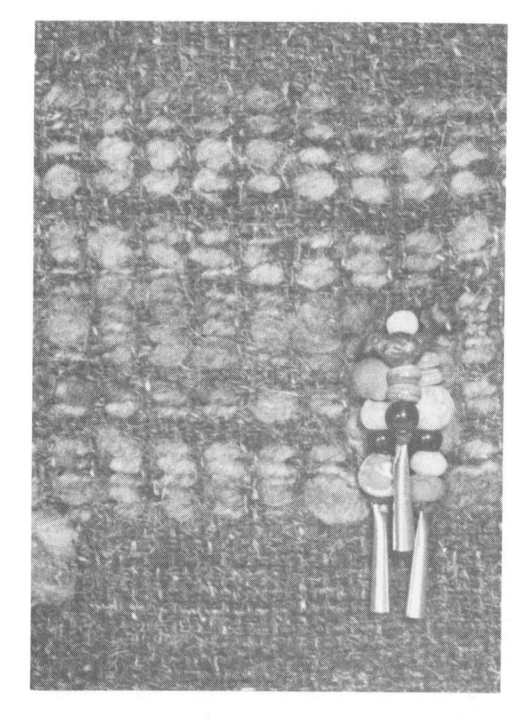

Detail of Bag #1: Dangles are antique glass beads, stoneware beads and tin cones.

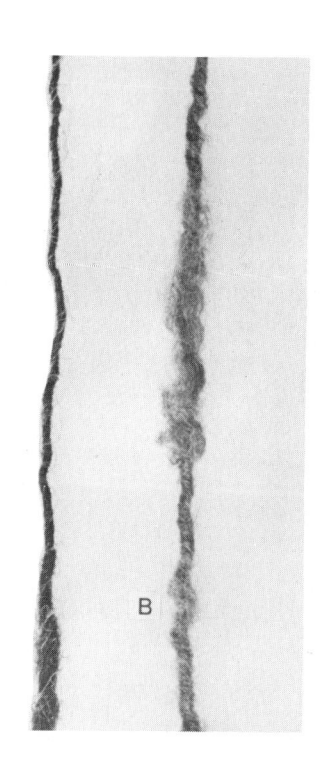

A Karakul.
B Gray wool.

Photographs by Nancy Piatkowsky   Bag #1: Inlay of handspun bulky wool.

inlay alternated randomly with rows of tabby. The dangle is a combination of antique glass and stoneware beads and tin cones.

The design area of Bag #2 was done with multiple strands of the bulky gray. A square was laid in under the dangle. Locks of a very coarse white/gray karakul were inlaid followed by more of the bulky gray. The dangles on this bag are a combination of the same glass and stoneware beads and tin cones as on Bag #1 with the addition of vertically drilled sea urchin spines.

The handles for both bags were made from six pieces of commercial rug wool wrapped with the handspun karakul. For comfort when using, this core was split at the shoulder into three parts. Each part was wrapped for about four inches and then brought back together. The handles were wrap-sewn to the bags for about two inches. The ends were pulled to the inside, knotted and sewn to the seam allowance.

The bags were interfaced with medium weight pellon. A zipper was sewn in the top by machine and a lining was handsewn to the zipper tape.

NOTE: After the material was taken from the loom, the raw ends were zig-zagged on the sewing machine and hand washed. Minimum shrinkage occurred. After a severe steam pressing they were assembled.

The finished size: 10" x 12".

Detail of Bag #2: Inlay bulky gray wool, karakul fleece dangle on either side of beads.

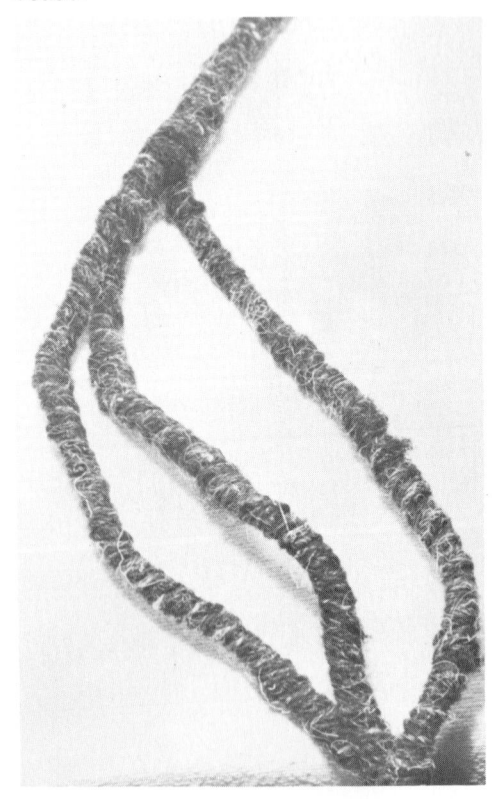

Detail: handle split at shoulder for comfort.

#2: Karakul, spun without carding.

JEAN LINDSTRAND BARTOS • Ketchikan, Alaska
CLARENCE M. LINDSTRAND • Roundup, Montana
Handwoven Coat of Handspun Wool

My grandmother brought her spinning wheel with her from Sweden in 1888. When I was growing up, it occupied a prominent place in our living room, even though no one used it. My father had learned to spin as a child, and when he retired in 1963, he finally had time to devote to it again. Some of the fleeces he used were from Columbia sheep belonging to the man who bought our ranch; the rest were from my uncle's Cheviot Cross flock. When Dad gave me a large amount of handspun, I just had to do something special and lasting with it!

A coat fabric seemed a logical choice, and I began by picking a pattern. Vogue #1023 had the simple elegant lines that would allow the fabric to be the focal point. The next problem was

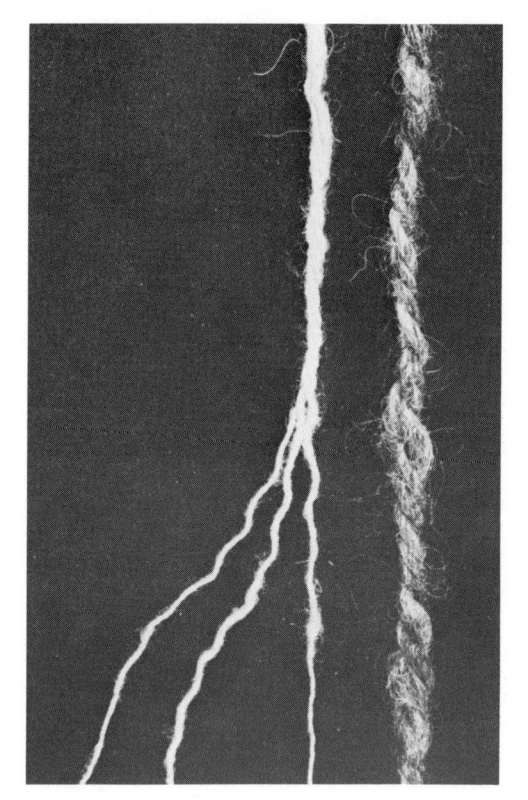

Three ply wool.

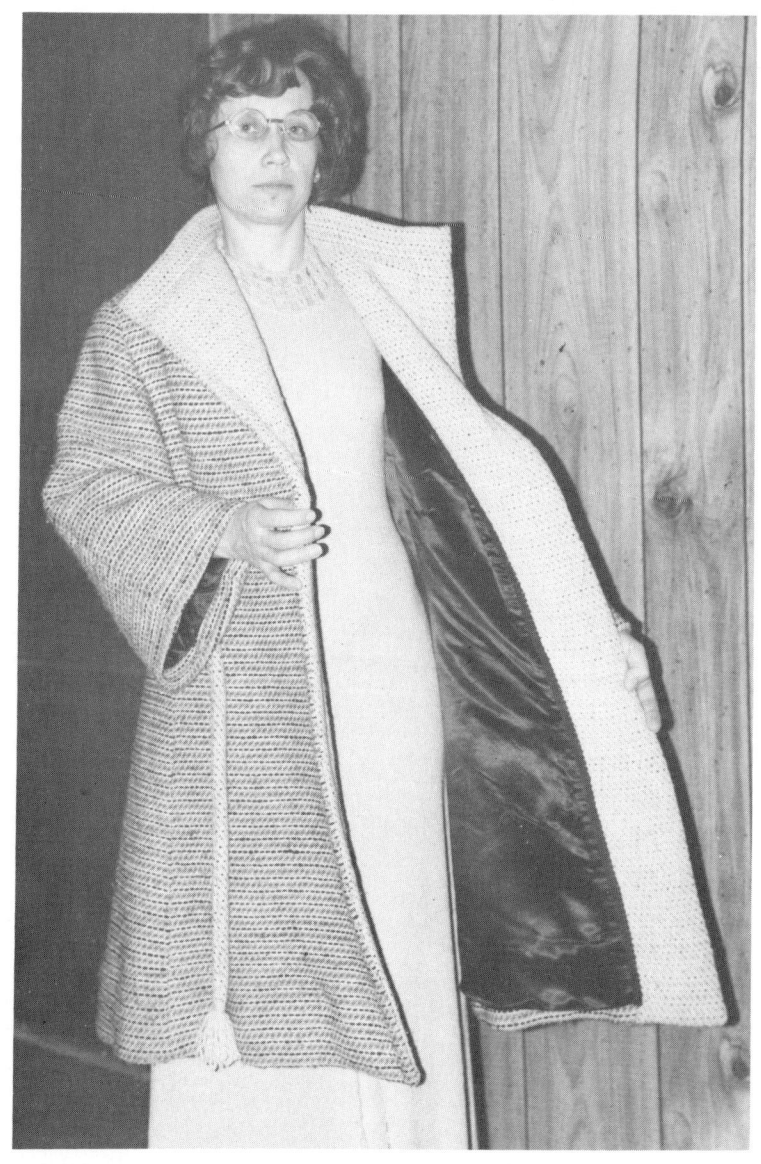

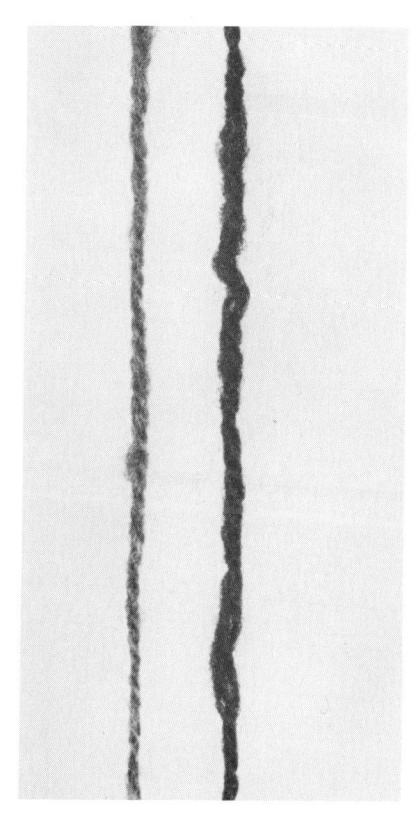

Three ply wool.

Photograph by Louis Bartos
Coat: handwoven yardage, handspun weft yarns.

51

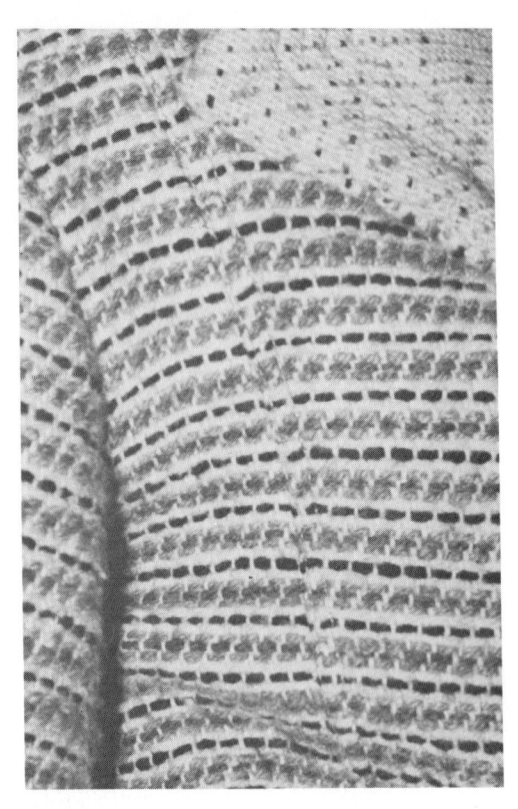

choosing a weaving pattern. Since I wanted the natural colors of the homespun to be more important than the pattern, I chose to use a three-and-one twill. Single shots of each of the four colors were used to avoid a definite striped look. Once I began weaving, I found that a tabby weft was necessary to stabilize the weave and give it body. This had an unexpected result . . . a double-faced fabric! The belt, collar, and facings were made to show the reverse side of the fabric.

Information on the weaving follows — the amounts of yarn are estimates.

Sett:	8 ends per inch	
Warp:	Bartlettsyarn heavy wool single warp 36 inches wide, 8 yards long	1½ pounds
Weft:	Pattern-natural colors of wool	4-5 pounds
	Tabby-Bartlettsyarn fine wool singles	1 pound
Finished Fabric:	After washing and steam pressing was 33 inches by 6½ yards.	

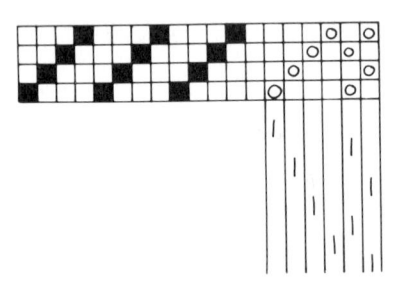

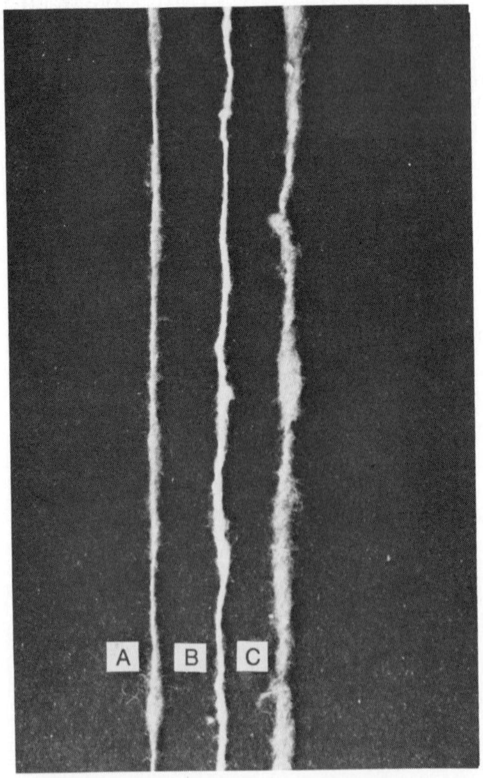

Close-up of collar, finishing on Jean Bartos coat.

A Baby camel down spun on wheel.
B,C Cashmere.

HOPE PARSHALL • Canoga Park, CA
Cashmere Scarves
Tote Bag
Hats

CASHMERE SCARVES

I had hoped to find a cashmere sweater while visiting the British Isles in 1977. When nothing seemed quite what I was looking for, I decided to search for cashmere yarn and knit my own. This too proved futile. Returning to the States, I tried again to find cashmere yarn; none was available anywhere. The obvious solution was to spin my own.

Just then a friend asked me to make her a scarf, as her neck and throat were particularly sensitive to the cold. Knowing that her skin was also sensitive, I showed her the cashmere and when she felt its luxurious softness, there was no question but that the scarf must be cashmere and not wool. I had no sooner finished hers than another woman asked me to make her one. Since I prefer to make each article different, I added in a stripe of baby camel hair, just as luxurious as the cashmere. One scarf uses two shades of cashmere, the other uses the same two shades of cashmere and the Mongolian baby camel.

Cashmere is truly a luxury item, particularly when you realize that a Kashmir goat will yield about half a pound a *year*.

As I understand it, they do not especially like to be combed for their undercoat, but camels take an even dimmer view of the procedure. In fact, the camel undercoat is collected during the moulting season by one man employed by the caravan. He walks at the rear, picking up the bits and pieces and stuffing them into a large bag. At the end of the journey it is sold in the marketplace.

Spinning cashmere is very easy, as it is usually beautifully clean and does not need to be carded or washed. I used the short draw, spinning a thin, single ply yarn.

Since I prefer to work solely in natural colors, I never dye any of my yarns. Kashmir goats come in a sort of oyster-shell white, a variety of browns and almost-black. The choice of colors was dictated by the fact that my source had only white and grey-brown at that time.

I knitted both the scarves in a basic ripple pattern, on size seven needles. My gauge was 7 sts = 1", 15 rows = 2". Pattern as follows:

Row 1: K1, K2 sts in the next st, K4, sl next st as if to purl, K2 tog, psso, K4 K2 sts in next st (14 sts in each group).
Row 2: Purl across.

I cast on 70 sts, separating each 14 sts with a ring marker. See photographs for striping. Each thin Mongolian baby camel and

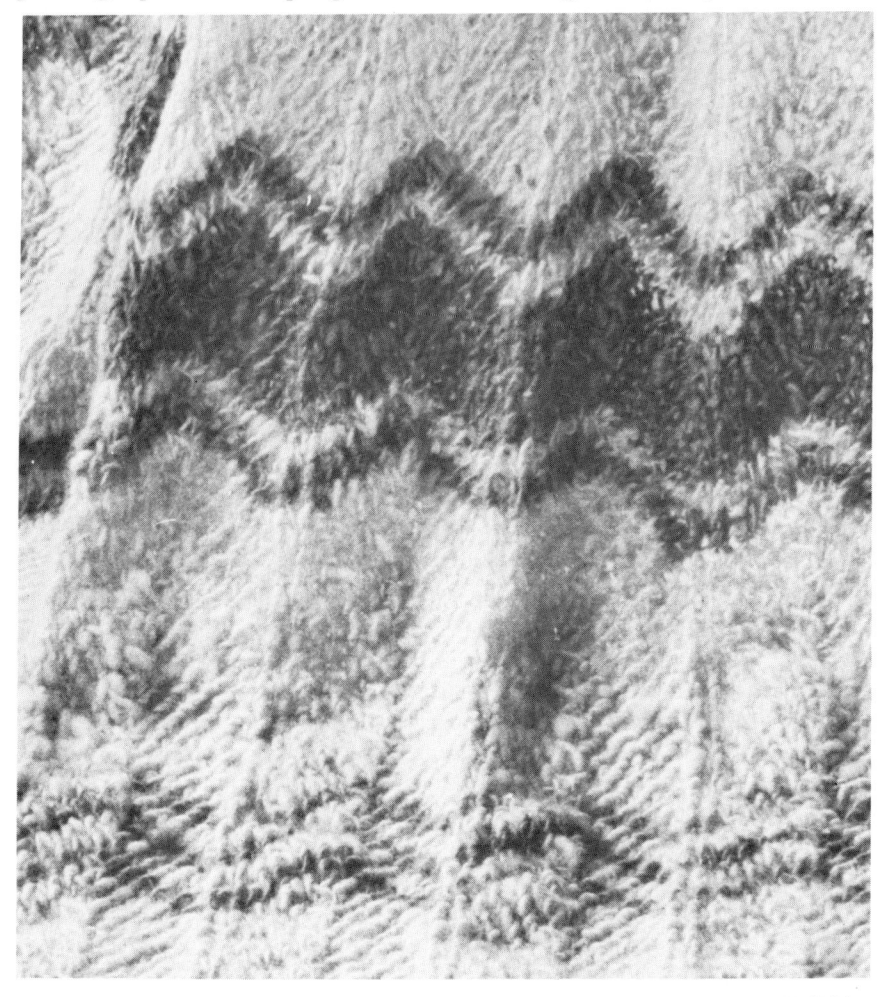

Cashmere from:

Studio of Handcrafts
P.O. Box 686
5405 Aura Avenue
Tarzana, CA 91356

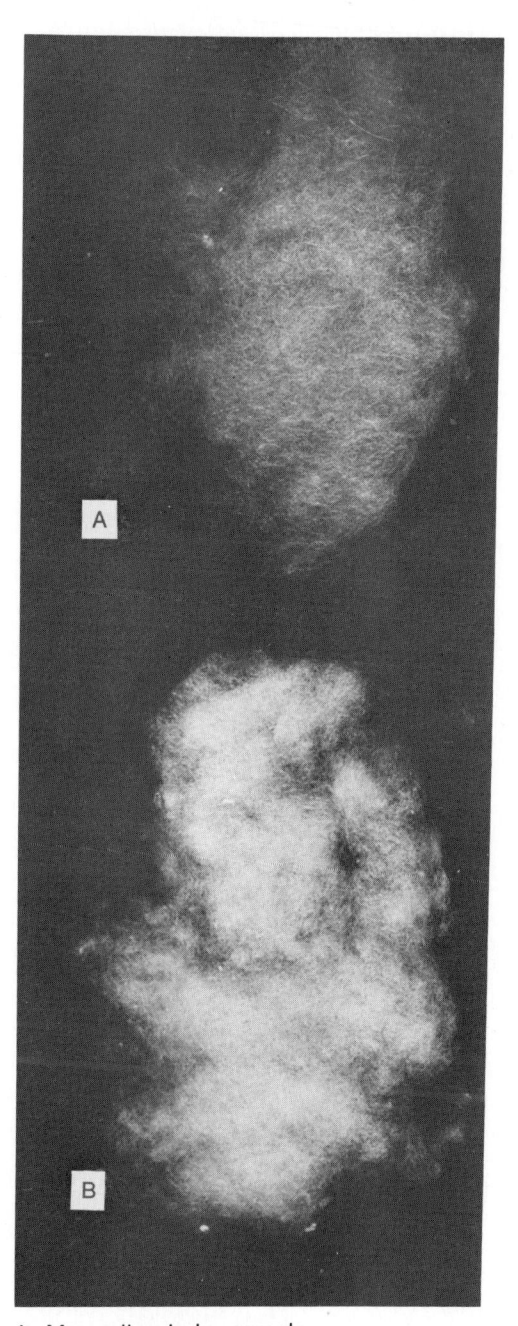

Detail of scarves. Fine, handspun yarn.   Photograph by Randy McBride.

A Mongolian baby camel.
B Chinese cashmere.

Scarves knitted in ripple pattern using cashmere and baby camel down. Incredibly soft and light.

Photograph by Randy McBride

Photograph by Randy McBride

Tote bag woven with handspun wool plied with novelty yarn on cotton warp.

white cashmere stripe is 2 rows (1 pattern, 1 purl). The wide grey-brown stripes are 8 rows (4 pattern alternating with 4 purl). The larger white dividing areas are 16 rows (8 pattern, 8 purl).

Anything made from these fibers should be handled carefully. Wash in tepid water with Ivory soap or Woolite; roll in a towel. Do NOT stretch. Squeeze excess water out. Carefully lay out to dry. Can also be dry-cleaned, if you prefer.

TOTE BAG

I had always been fascinated by novelty yarns. This project evolved out of a desire to learn to spin with a controlled slub.

I used a white Rambouillet wool because the long staple made it easier for a beginning spinner to create a controlled slub. I plyed my handspun with a thin green thread that has tiny flecks of red, blue, and pale yellow in it.

The loom was threaded with a lightweight cotton warp at 10 epi, using a 10 dent reed. The entire bag was woven in tabby, depending on stripes for the pattern effect.

STRIPING:

1½" green
1" white
3 rows of white, looping wool over a fat dowel
2½" white
3 rows red
1¾" green
3 rows red
5" white
3 rows red
2" green
3 rows red
Balance white
Ending with 1½" green stripe

Controlled slub plied with commercial novelty yarn.

Photograph by Randy McBride

Close-up of tote bag, note loops made over dowel.

To finish the bag I crocheted two strips of white 6 sts wide in treble crochet long enough to use as side inserts. The bag is lined in off-white velour, with side inserts to fit. I use handles that can be slipped out and used with various bags. The final finishing was done by hand.

HATS

The hat in the foreground was my very first project after I learned to spin. The other hat was made because I was fascinated by the complexities of the pattern, and also wanted to experiment with blending wools into heather shades.

Hat number one was made of white Rambouillet wool; dark brown and charcoal wool from New Zealand, purchased from Rita Dayton. I spun using a long draw and left the yarn single ply. The hat took a total of about 3 oz of yarn. Knitting was done on double-pointed needles, size 5 and size 2, both 10" long.

Pattern as follows:

Pattern is K2, P2 throughout.
Cast on 96 sts. K2, P2 for 6 inches.
Change color and knit new color on, then return on next row to K2, P2. Continue in pattern for ½", about 6 rows.
Change to main color and knit this on. Next row return to pattern of K2, P2 for ¾".
Change to color for 2nd stripe, knit on. Next row K2, P2 for ½".
Change to main color and proceed as before for ¾".
Change to color for 3rd stripe, knit on; next row K2, P2 for ½".
Return to main color, knit on; next row continue K2, P2 pattern for a few rows.
Change to No. 2 needles and continue in pattern until piece measures 9½".

Rita Dayton
Box 887
Simi Valley, CA 93065

Hats of handspun wool. Hat in foreground knitted on double-pointed needles. Yarn for second hat is blend of three shades of wool roving carded together.

Photograph by Randy McBride

Next row, K2 tog all the way around (32 sts).
Next row, K1, P1.
Next row, K2 tog all the way around (16 sts).
Next row, K1, P1.
Next row, K2 tog all the way around (8 sts).
Leaving long thread, gather the 8 sts with a needle and pull together; secure firmly.
Make pompom, if desired.

It is very simple to use commercial patterns with handspun yarns, particularly hat patterns. Just be sure to duplicate the gauge. Hat number two is an example of a commercial pattern adapted to handspun yarns. The heather effect is created by carding three shades of commercially dyed roving together. I lay small bits of the three colors across the carder and proceed to card very gently. The final result will be a soft mixture of your colors that is quite different from any of the colors that you started with. It is rather like painting with wool.

ROSE PERL • Auburn, California

Knitted Vest

The fleece was a gift from a friend who had a pet sheep. When the sheep died shortly after the shearing it seemed appropriate to use the wool to make a garment for my friend. The yarn is 2 ply with a loose twist to keep it as soft as possible. It was spun in the grease in spite of being extremely oily, then washed to remove some of the oil and dirt. A final wash, after the garment was completed, got out the rest.

I experimented with several sizes of knitting needles and crochet hooks, with various patterns until the right one emerged. The yarn was too thick for crochet. It worked well for knitting if I used a rather large needle. Finally a sample was made to obtain the gauge. Then working from my friend's hip size (plus a bit more for good measure) I adjusted the number of stitches to the pattern repeat, which is a multiple of four plus one.

Directions are for medium size.

#13 knitting needles   J crochet hook
Gauge: 8 sts per 3"; 4 rows per 1"

Pattern: Row 1: P1, K3. Repeat, ending with P1.
Row 2: Purl across.

Start with 89 sts. Work evenly about 18" or desired length to underarm. Decrease for neck and armhole: On knit side, decrease first st by knitting 2 tog. Continue in pattern for 18 sts more. Purl the last 2 sts tog (22 sts worked). This is the right front. Turn and purl across as usual. Decrease one st every 6th row on neck edge four more times. At the same time decrease at armhole side every other row 2 more times. Work 9½" from first decrease or desired length (14 sts remaining). Cast off.

Photographs by Patricia Thaxter.

Rose modeling knitted vest. This is a good project for a novice knitter—quick and easy.

Rose is currently the owner of:

The Craft Shop
Route 2, Box 121A
Willow Springs, MO 65793

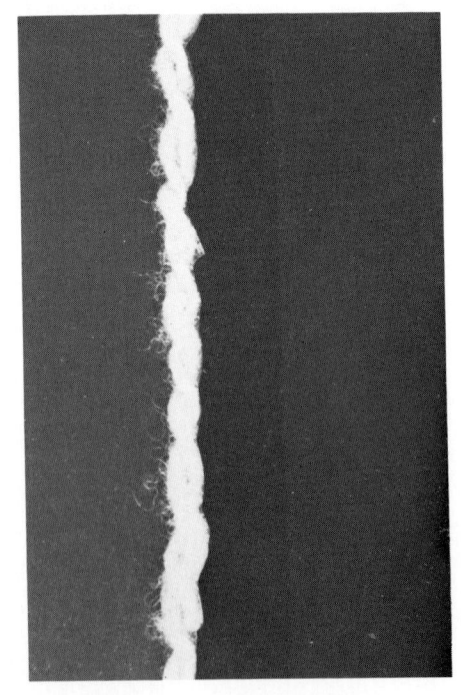

Two ply wool.

Work left front to match, except at neck decrease. If 2nd from last st is purl, purl the last 2 tog. If a knit st, then slip the st, knit last st, and psso.

Back: (45 sts) Decrease first and last st. Purl one row. Decrease first and last st once more. Continue for same length as front. Cast off. Sew shoulder seams. With J hook crochet 2 rows of single crochet around edge. Crochet one row of single crochet around armhole.

ROZ SHIRLEY • Los Gatos, California
"Desert Sun"
"Crocheted Basket with Eggs"

"DESERT SUN"
Wallhanging on Cholla Cactus 4' high by 6' long

"Desert Sun" was a commissioned wall hanging. The McAlisters had seen my work and they had a cholla cactus branch on which they wanted a weaving. After meeting with them to discover their tastes in colors and techniques, I did a series of sketches of ideas. The McAlisters approved one and my work began.

One truism that I've learned is that there is no way to really plan an off-loom weaving or sculptural crochet. I may have a good idea of how I want the work to progress, but during the actual application, find that things must change in order to preserve the essence of the idea. Or, sometimes the idea must evolve because a more interesting or exciting development has begun. Lately, when I'm not sure how to do something, given the limitations of the materials, I find that if I say "What if ...?" a solution will present itself fairly soon. Sometimes I work around the materials, and sometimes I discover that the materials — and I — are not as limited as I thought. That whole concept opens up all sorts of new worlds!

The fibers used in "Desert Sun" are mostly my own handspun yarns, both natural and dyed. However, I also used a rust rug yarn from Craft Yarns of Rhode Island, and some mohair (handspun in South Africa) which I found at Custom Handweavers. I started with New Zealand greasy carded wool, colored and white, purchased from Mountain Weaver, and used a Paragon wheel, made by Craig Rehbein to spin it. I deliberately spun a thick and thin "homespun" type yarn to create interest in the texture of the finished piece.

Knowing the colors wanted for the final design, I chose to use a coralline dye. Following my general work routine, I premordanted yarn in one-pound lots, four skeins to the pound and used alum, tin, chrome, copper and iron mordants. I put half a pound of coralline wood shavings in a nylon net bag and soaked the shavings for about two hours in hot water to start the color running. Then I added 1¼ pounds of wetted yarn (one skein from each of the mordants) and slowly brought the dye pot to a simmer, holding it at that temperature for about an hour. I let the yarn set in the dye bath until cool enough to handle. In order to obtain a more extended palette of colors, the

Vest knitted by Rose Perl. Handspun 2-ply wool.

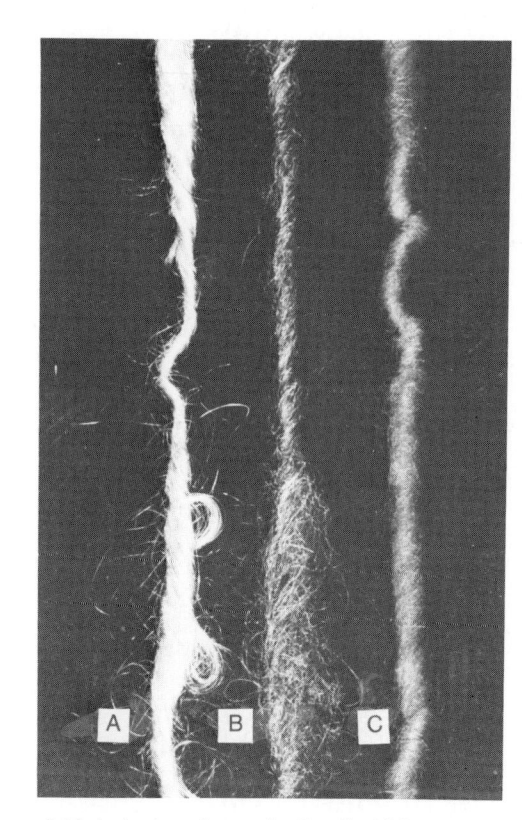

A Mohair, handspun in South Africa.
B New Zealand wool.
C New Zealand wool, naturally dyed.

Custom Handweavers
Allied Arts Guild
Arbor Road and Creek Drive
Menlo Park, CA 94025

Mountain Weaver
P.O. Box 1734
334 N. Santa Cruz
Los Gatos, CA 95030

The Mannings
R.D.2
East Berlin, PA 17316

To crochet around hoop: make a slip knot, go under and through the center of the hoop with the hook, catch the yarn with the hook, bring it back through the hoop towards you,

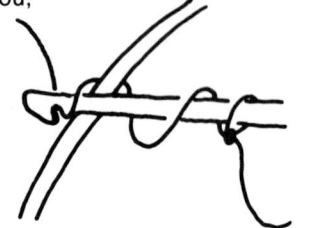

go up and over the hoop, catch the yarn

and bring it through the two loops on the hook. Pull tight.

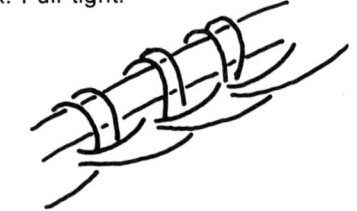

Pack stitches tightly.

Also shown in color.

entire dye process was then repeated with a pot of fresh water and more of the wetted, pre-mordanted yarn, but with the same coralline. These colors were much softer than those from the first dye bath. The coralline was purchased at Mountain Weaver, but they are unfortunately no longer a source of this lovely dyestuff. Try the Mannings, in Pennsylvania.

To begin the work of carrying out the design I crocheted around metal hoops so that I could anchor the warps which crossed in the centers of the hoops. The commercial rug yarn was used for wrapping and warps. After weaving on the warped hoops I had to figure out how to secure them to the cactus. The small hoop was to be attached directly to the cactus, wedged between two branches. Cholla cactus is marvelous — it has holes to loop yarn through! I used a curved needle to thread the yarn into the cactus then back out through another hole. Then I threaded the yarn through the crocheted edge of the woven hoop, pulled it tight, and went back through the cactus holes until I felt that edge was *really* secure. This was repeated wherever the hoop touched the cactus. The large hoop was suspended from a subsidiary branch and anchored, to keep it from swinging or turning, by yarn cords to the main branch and also to another part of the subsidiary branch. I threaded the yarn through the cactus holes as explained above — but did not pull the yarn tight after threading through the crocheted hoop edge because I wanted the hoop suspended between the two branches — not snug against them. I did not tie off the yarn until after I had secured the hoop from the bottom and was happy with the placement of the hoop in the space. Then I added the "anchor lines" at the side so the hoop would be stable. All these "anchor lines" were ugly — so I grouped them and wrapped each grouping with the rust commercial yarn. Finally, I added the hanging groups of handspuns by threading

Photographs by Mary Ellen Schultz.

Large hoop. Note slits, wrapped cords, finishing of center. Woven from outside in.

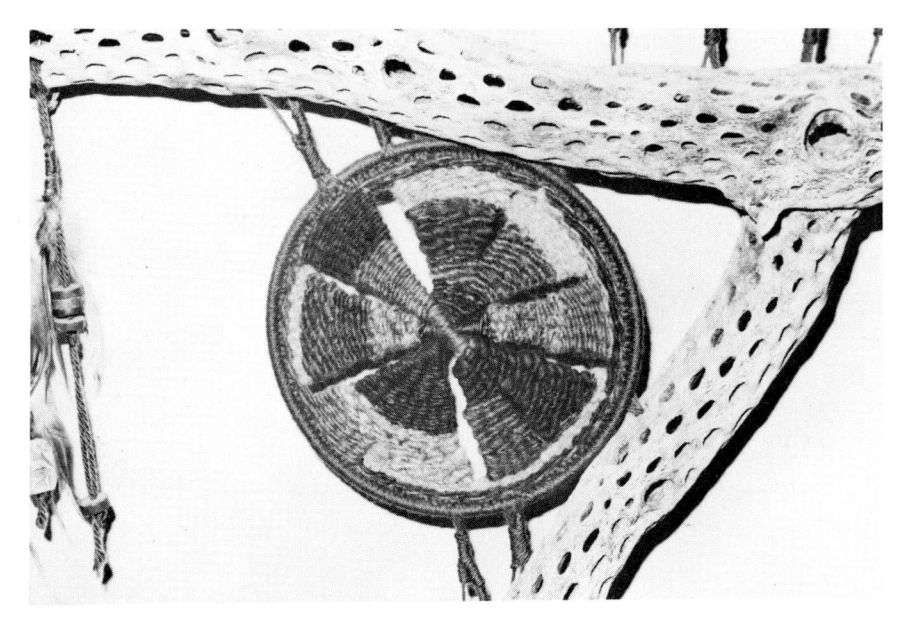

Smaller shield, fits snugly against branches of cactus.

through the holes in the cactus and securing the yarns with overhand knots. Then I added groups of bauxite beads to some yarns, and feathers to others.

Basically the weaving was American Indian in feeling — somewhat reminiscent of shields — yet there was nothing traditional about the idea, the yarns or the techniques.

"CROCHETED BASKET WITH EGGS"
4½" high by 9½" long by 8" wide

The basket is an irregularly shaped, self-supporting container. Basically, it just grew as I crocheted. The wire eggs evolved because the container looked rather bored until I gave it something to hold. The basket is also unique in that several natural dyes were used, including onion skins. My husband proudly came home one day with several bags of onion skins. He had collected about 50 pounds by going to a field where onions were being given away because the field was going to be plowed under. Everyone else wanted the onions — he wanted the skins. So he collected onions for people in exchange for the skins — and I have some gorgeous yarn!

The fibers used in this piece were: "Curlama" made by Stanley Berroco; heavy gray yarn made by Menlo Woolen Mills; steel gray mohair which I spun from roving purchased at Mountain Weaver; hairy pinkish-tan yarn I spun from a white karakul fleece obtained in the grease from Santa Cruz Weavers Supply; the remaining handspun yarns which I spun from Corriedale Fleeces purchased from Haber/Zemel/Tryon Wool Market in S. San Francisco. The jute used was 3 ply, quite lightweight. For the eggs, I used different weights of wire so that some are very firm and others feel soft and resilient. Copper wire is found in coils at any hardware store or garden supply store. Aluminum (or steel) wire and brass wire are found on

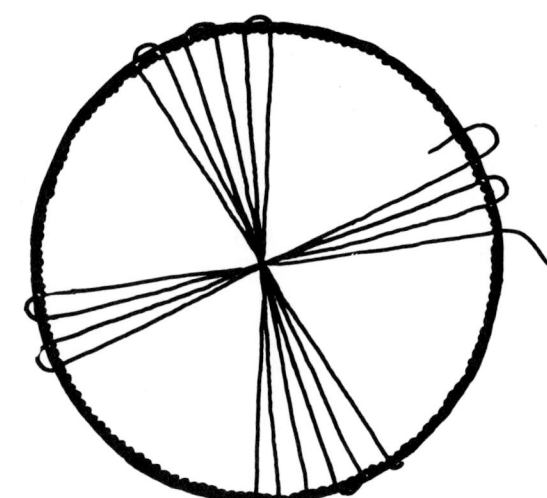

Warping: Be careful of tension—the hoop can distort as you move around the circle. One solution is to warp this way then fill in the sections. The warp builds up in the center, but *after* the hoop is woven you can wrap portions of the center warps for an interesting effect (small sketch). Have an uneven number of warp threads if possible — especially if you want to weave bands of color leading towards the center. This is not as important if you are planning to weave sections and slits.

Weaving: Do 3 or 4 rows of tabby in either the color of the warping on the hoop or the base color (the one that sets the color tones of the whole weaving). Pack down. It is helpful to temporarily tie the center warp threads. Use a different short length of yarn or string for each tie. Best way is to pinch the warp closed with thumb and forefinger of one hand while slipping the tie yarns into place. Just fasten with a simple bowknot.

Now start weaving. The photos show that I broke my circle into segments of varying widths by using the slot technique. Some segments also utilized slits which went part of the length of the segment before being woven back together to make a single pie-shaped segment. Most of the weaving was done in tabby, varied occasionally by going over two threads, under one.

61

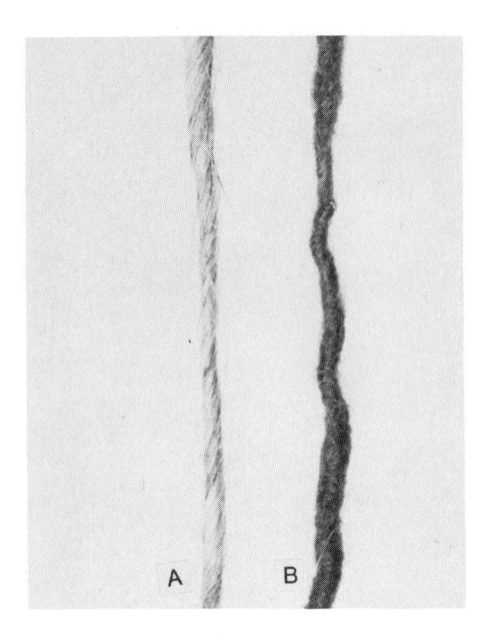

A Mohair, from roving.
B Wool, dyed with acorns.

Santa Cruz Weaver's Supply
1001 Center Street
P.O. Box 1294
Santa Cruz, CA 95061

Haber/Zemel/Tryon Wool
325 Harbor Way
South San Francisco, CA 94080

Earth Guild/Grateful Union
Mail Order Service
Hot Springs, NC 28743

Straw Into Gold
5533 College Avenue
Oakland, CA 94618

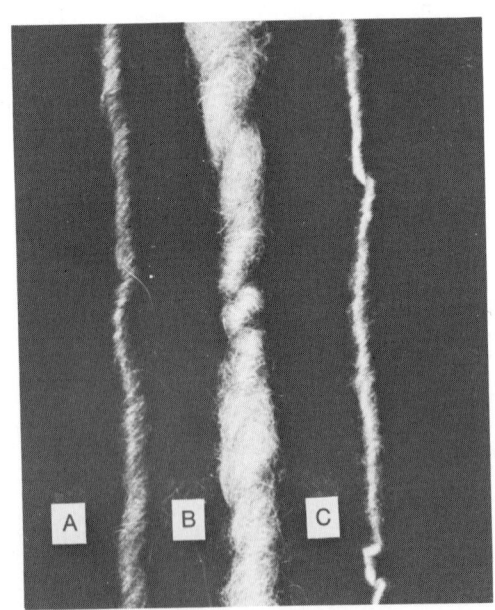

A Karakul.
B,C Corriedale.

Detail of basket   Photograph by Mary Ellen Schultz

small spools at hardware stores.

After purchasing the fleeces, I sorted them, discarding what couldn't be used because of felting, dirt or barnyard material. Then I washed them and spun the wool into yarn on a Paragon wheel made by Craig Rehbein. The yarns are rough textured, which I like for the lovely feel they give, and because they are sturdier when crocheted.

All the dyed yarns were processed in a direct dye bath, i.e., the pre-mordanted yarn was added to the water along with the dye materials, then the temperature was slowly brought to a simmer and held there for approximately one hour. The one exception was the acorn dye bath. I cracked about 3 pounds of acorns, covered them with hot water and let them set for 2 days. Then I added one pound of yarn which had been pre-mordanted with iron, brought it to a simmer and cooked everything for one hour. The yarn set overnight before being rinsed and hung to dry.

The following are my sources of natural dye materials: A handy oak tree. Mountain Weaver, The Mannings, Earth Guild, Straw Into Gold. Any person who likes to carve or whittle with exotic woods (all the scraps, barks can be accumulated until there is enough for a dye pot). A husband and an onion field.

Now that my collection of strange yarns was complete I began to crochet the basket. Start by chaining five or six stitches, then join to first chain to make a circle. Work two stitches in each of the original chain — use single, half-double or double — whatever you feel like and as irregularly as you want. When the base looks finished, stop increasing the number of stitches and the sides will begin to take shape. To make interesting lumps — and a sturdy container — I crocheted with a hook which was too small for the yarns used. Sometimes I left a hole, then filled it in with a tightly crocheted half-sphere (roughly) that could either bulge out or fold in on itself. I would crochet back and forth in one area to build it up, then join in another yarn to flow around the shape. The basket is finished when it feels right.

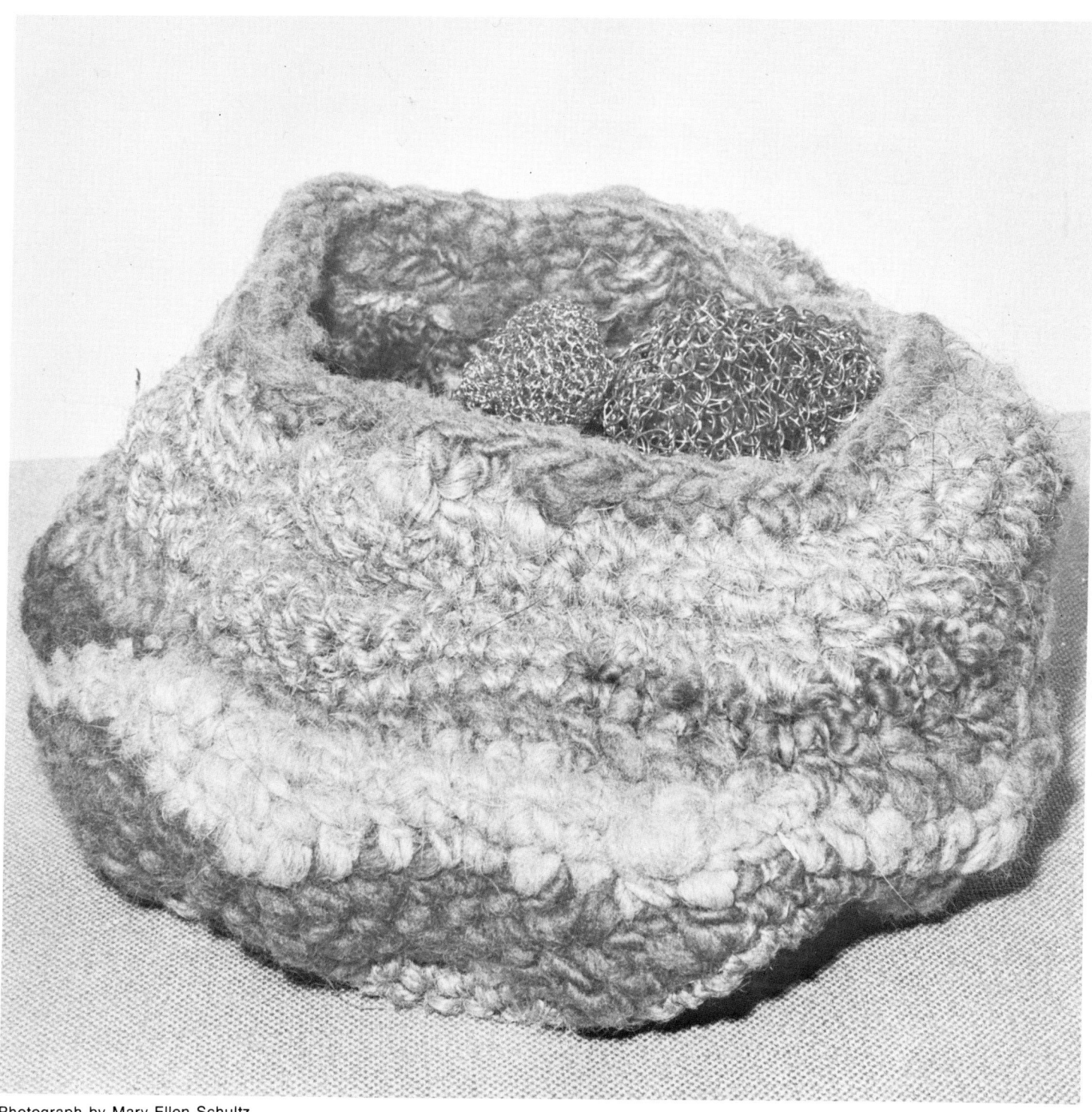

Photograph by Mary Ellen Schultz

"Crocheted Basket with Eggs." Handspun wool, naturally dyed yarns. Jute adds sturdiness.

Unlined knit jacket, yarn spun thick and thin.

ELSIE EWBANK • Warsaw, Kentucky
Three sweaters

I have been spinning five years and all the wool that I use is from our flock of sheep. We maintain 150 to 175 ewes and lamb them out and do all the necessary work in a family operation. One third of our fleece is hand sorted and sacked separately for handspinning. My husband, daughter, and I all spin and weave.

The man's jacket is unlined, but very heavy and suitable to wear outdoors in the coldest weather. It also works well as a sport jacket, or with casual clothes. The jacket is made from two ply yarn spun from pure bred Dorset ram's fleece, medium staple 2½ to 3½ inches. The yarn is very coarse and used up the good wool from two years' fleeces (20 pounds gross).

Most of the yarn was spun on the walking wheel (great wheel) as I learned to spin; however, I progressed to a finer thread before I had completed enough for the jacket. I found I could duplicate the yarn by just lightly carding on large toothed tow cards leaving many tangles and some of the debris to be removed later in washing. In the actual spinning to achieve the "beginner" effect I found that the most successful way was to use the walking wheel and to draft very little. This can also be managed on an Ashford or saxony wheel by not drafting, just allowing the wheel to separate the wool as it comes from your hand. A clean, picked fleece can be spun this way without carding.

The jacket is knit in a plain knit on size 17 needles. The pattern was used as a reference only for length and shaping. The

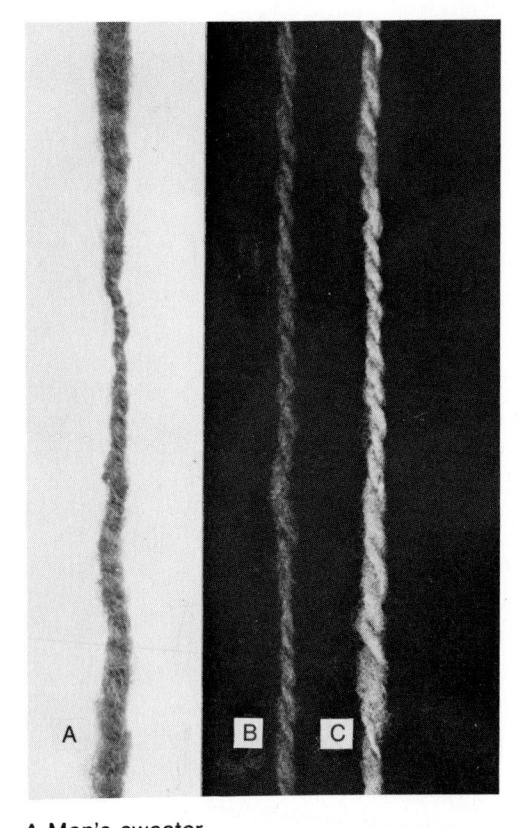

A Man's sweater.
B Child's sweater.
C Mock cable sweater.

Detail of man's jacket.

Photographs by Sandra Wallin

sleeves are set in in a square arm's eye as a focal point and the collar stands up, but away from the neck allowing a comfortable fit over a dress or sport shirt.

The knitting on the jacket and both children's sweaters was done by Jean Pryor of Georgetown, Kentucky. Jean is a "super knitter" having knit socks, sweaters, coats, vest, hats, gloves, etc. for her family of six for over twenty years. On all the pieces she was of unbelievable help. Her experience with various yarns and patterns was so instinctive that she was able to look at a type of handspun and say what would or would not work for a given style or pattern. My advice to anyone wanting to spin yarn for a certain project would be to find an experienced knitter, if you are not one, to advise. Spin about 2 ounces of yarn in the manner you are planning to use and have your "knitter" work with it and see if it is suitable for your project.

The smaller children's sweater, size six, was knitted in a medium fine spun 2-ply yarn made from a ewe's fleece of approximately eight pounds gross. The yarn is *slightly* underspun in areas which gives a soft look but the plying adds the necessary strength and stability. Most of it was spun on an Ashford wheel. It was knit on size 8 needles in a rib knit with a cowl collar and raglan sleeves which allow for growing. One child got three years' wear from this garment and it will now be passed on to younger nieces and nephews. It zips so it is suitable for either boys or girls. A matching stocking cap was knitted from the extra yarn which makes a striking outfit for dress or sports wear.

Close-up of child's sweater shows detail of rib pattern.

Child's sweater with knitted cap. Medium fine 2 ply handspun on Ashford wheel.

Three sweaters, yarn by Elsie Ewbank, knitting by Jean Pryor.

The third sweater is knit in a mock-cable pattern in a girl's size 14-16 cardigan, with a matching tam. The yarn was spun from a ewe's fleece of medium-long staple, gross weight ten pounds. This ewe is the result of a three way cross including Dorset, Suffolk, and Western ewes. Twenty-six ounces of washed two-ply was spun and used in this garment. The yarn was spun finely and uniformly, on a Finnish castle wheel, to allow the pattern to be the focal point of this outfit, rather than the yarn. Handmade pottery buttons were used on the stockinette band for finishing.

My experience has been that the simpler patterns make more striking garments in homespun, allowing the yarn to be the focal point of hand-knit pieces. Natural closings, either bone, antler, or pottery buttons, lap and tie, or zippers are most attractive. Natural dyes seem to be the most complimentary to handspun wools.

Mock-cable sweater: yarn was spun more evenly than for the other two sweaters.

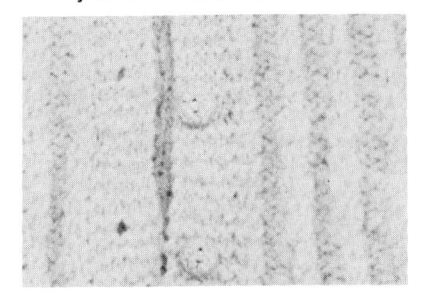

Detail of mock cable sweater. Buttons are handmade pottery.

JUDI CLARK • Westminster, Maryland
Superblanket II

Superblanket II is a bed cover. It covers a double bed amply enough for two persons to comfortably share it. It is made of yarn handspun of wool, alpaca and mohair. Like its smaller predecessor, Superblanket I, it provides instant warmth.

SB II was woven in two pieces. The long narrow piece was cut and joined selvage-wise to the selvage edges of the short, wide piece.

Actual time spent on the blanket amounted to less than a month, full-time. However, the effort managed to spread itself over three years.

Actual cost of the blanket must be between $25 and $40. I have much fleece and yarn left over and cannot estimate more closely than that.

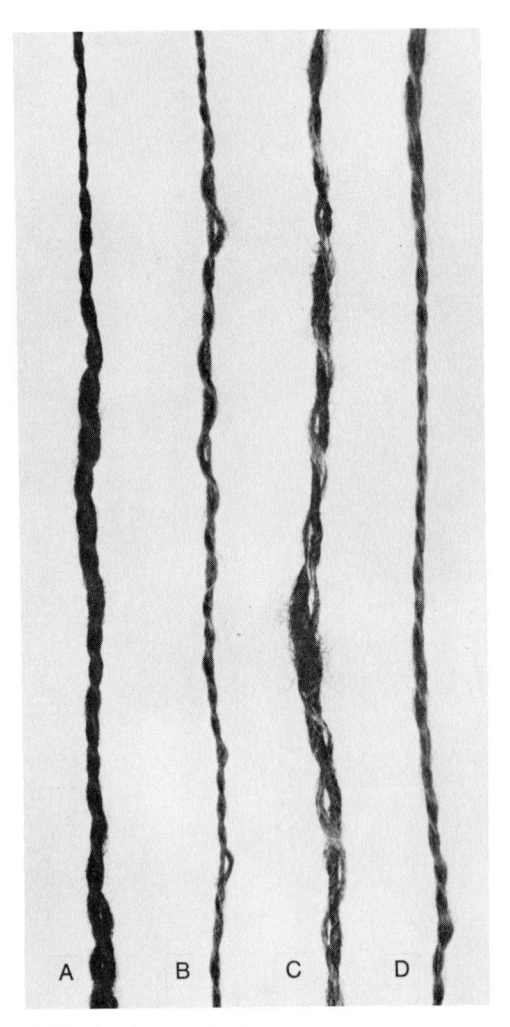

A Black alpaca, 2 ply.
B Brown mohair plied with wool from Denise.
C Grey alpaca plied with wool from Denise.
D Brown mohair, 2 ply.

Superblanket II. All handspun yarns. The blanket is very thick and extremely warm.

Photograph by Dick Cheatham

The fibers used were:

Grey
Wool: purchased for me by a friend at a farm in Vermont.
Alpaca: purchased as roving from a booth at the Northern California Weaver's Conference, Turlock, CA, Spring, 1972

Brown
Wool: from "Denise," a sheep whose fleece was sold at the New England Weaver's Seminar, Amherst, MA, Summer, 1975
Mohair: purchased at the Mannings, East Berlin, PA
Alpaca: "Short Staple," purchased from Scott's Woolen Mill, Uxbridge, MA

Black
Wool: Speilslau fleece, purchased at Cider Mill Weaving Studio, Bernardston, MA
Alpaca: purchased at the Mannings, East Berlin, PA

White
Wool: Romney fleece, sheep raised and shorn by Bob and Beth (Gilden-) Watrous, Cider Mill Weaving Studio, Bernardston, MA
Mohair: purchased at New England Weaver's Seminar, Amherst, MA, Summer, 1975

Scott's Woolen Mill
Hecia Street and Elmdale Road
Uxbridge, Massachusetts 01569

In general, as little processing was done as possible. The alpaca and mohair arrived as marvelous roving requiring nothing more than division into manageable lengths for spinning. I generally pull off staple-length pieces to spin, folding the roving lengths over my middle finger and drawing from the bend in the roving.

The grey wool was washed prior to purchase, and matted enough to require picking and carding. Members of the Wool Gatherers, a Western Massachusetts spinning group, helped me with this.

The brown wool required only flicking until it dried up, at which point I oiled the fleece prior to flicking (see oiling recipe).

The black Speilslau fleece required carding because it has both a long hair-like fiber and a short down-like fiber. It was clean and needed no washing.

The white Romney fleece required only flicking at first, until it, too, became dry and sticky as did the brown wool above. I soaked the Romney in the tub, then dried it and flick carded it. It didn't need oiling.

I plyed warp yarns as my fancy struck me, that is, the 7 dark fibers used resulted in many more than 7 warp yarns. The photos show samples of the warp yarns which seem most representative. The yarn appearance came out surprisingly uniform, considering the variety of fibers used. Mohair/mohair yarns are the smoothest and shiniest, whereas wool/wool yarns

Spinning Oil
(adapted from Deloria Chapin)

1/3 cup ammonia
1/3 cup salad oil
1 cup warm water

Mix together and store in glass jar.

Sprinkle fleece with oil mixture one to two days prior to carding. Only oil enough fleece for planned spinning. Finish and wash yarn within one week of oiling for best results, as the fibers become gummy with time. Oil should make fiber handling easier, faster and much more enjoyable.

Warp for Superblanket II on loom. Warp is a
mixture of handspun 2 ply yarns. Usually
one ply is alpaca or mohair, the other strand wool.

are the fuzziest and dullest. Alpaca/wool yarns are light and fuzzy, without the shine of mohair. (I didn't try plying alpaca and mohair.)

I plyed my warp yarns before washing any of the fibers, even though I realized the wool would be apt to shrink more than the alpaca and mohair singles. I did this on purpose, reasoning that the yarn would fluff up better after the piece was woven if the plyed yarn contained singles of differing lengths. The only slip-up was that, somehow, I forgot to wash one of the plyed yarns. The unwashed yarn found its way into the very center of my blanket, and naturally, shrank when the entire blanket got its bath, resulting in an 11" difference between the center length of the piece and the selvage length of the piece. Steaming and another bath reduced the gross difference to 6", so that the final blanket lies fairly smooth on a bed.

Spinning was simple and straightforward. Singles were spun z-twist. Yarn was plyed s-twist. I used my Ashford wheel for most of the spinning. Part of the yarn was spun using a very fast Canadian wheel on loan from Ute Bargmann.

Superblanket II, as you might suspect, grew out of Superblanket I. SB I is a smaller lap robe, approximately 70% alpaca. I decided to make a larger, bed-size version many years ago, soon after I finished the smaller blanket. SB I sheds fibers, and I decided to spin the yarns a little tighter, and weave the blanket a little closer for SB II. I also wanted to avoid the weight of 50-50 wool/mohair yarn such as I had used for SB I. So . . . SB II resulted, weighing approximately 8 pounds, and being composed of approximately 10% mohair, 35% alpaca, and 55% wool by weight. SB I was weft-faced both sides. SB II

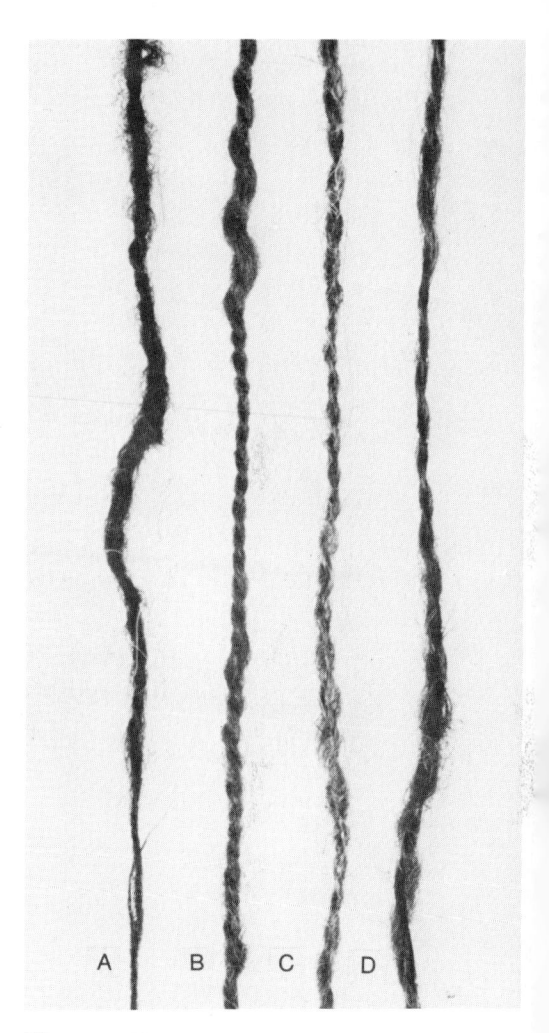

Warp yarns.
A Black Speilslau 2 ply.
B Brown alpaca plied with wool from Denise.
C Grey wool, 2 ply.
D Black Speilslau plied with wool from Denise.

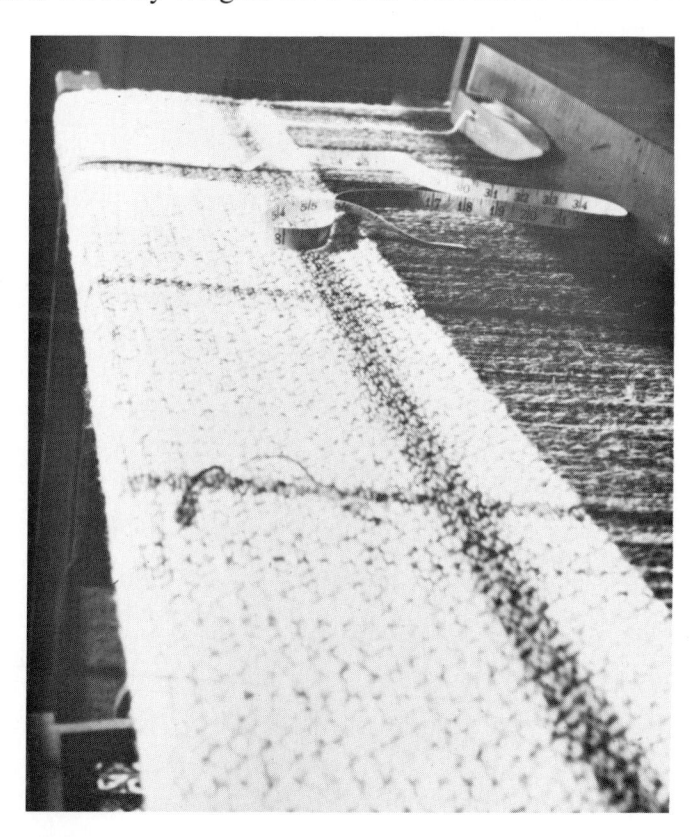

Weft face of blanket. Singles, handspun Romney fleece. Weave is a 3/1 point twill.

was woven in a kind of 3/1 point twill (see draft), so that it is weft-faced on one side, and warp-faced on the other.

The blanket was woven in two pieces on my 50" wide loom. The first piece went on the loom as 7½ yards, 26" wide. After finishing, it had shrunk down to 6½ yards, 21" wide.

The second piece went on the loom as 4 yards, 50" wide. After finishing, it had shrunk down to 41" wide, and 94" center length, 102" outside length (not including 3" fringe). The discrepancy in length for the wider center piece was due to my failure to prewash the yarns used in the center, a near disastrous oversight. Loom waste took approximately ½ yard of warp; fringe took approximately 6", cut down to 3½".

Warp was set at 12 epi, double in a 6 dent reed.

Weft was approximately 10 picks per inch. Weft yarns weighed nearly three pounds, warp yarns over five. I have a small square of cloth left over, approximately 20" by 20".

Total yarn yardage:	Estimated time involved:
4000 yards weft (singles) @ 200 yds/hr	20 hours
5000 yards warp (2 ply) @ 100 yds/hr	50 hours
9000 yards	70 hours
Weaving, including warping:	30 hours
Finishing:	8 hours
	108 hours

The above estimates might mislead one into thinking that such a project could be completed in less than three working weeks. That would be quite difficult. As it was, I developed calf cramps while jogging after all-day spinning sessions. The weaving and finishing actually stretched over much more time, since I was uncertain about what I was doing. In all, the entire Superblanket II took over three years to complete.

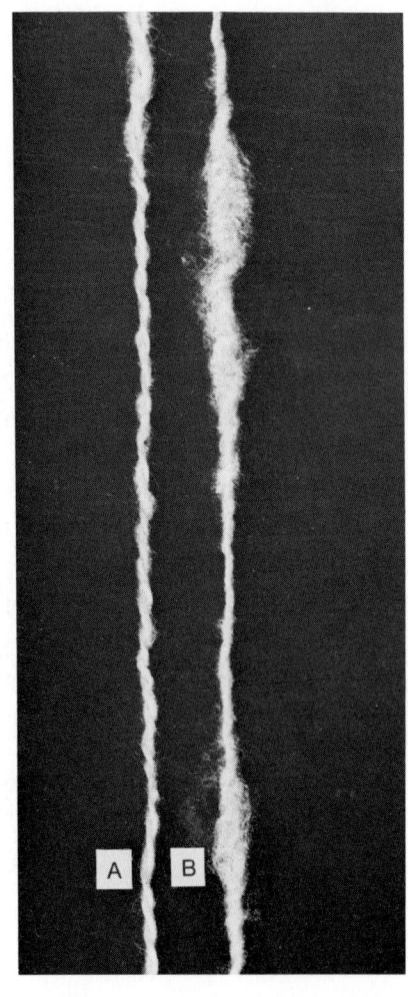

A Mohair plied with Romney wool.
B Weft, singles, Romney.

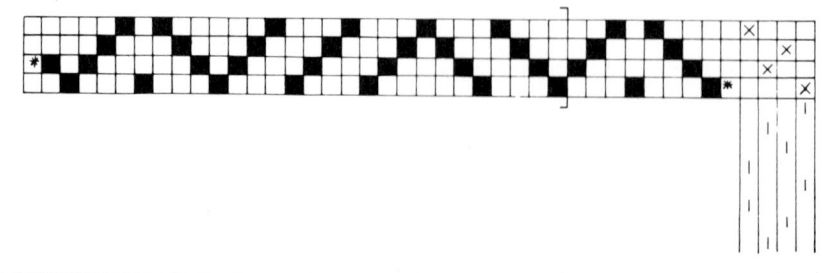

Superblanket II. Detail of weave.   Photograph by Dick Cheatham

JOAN SIEGEL • Stout, Ohio
Mable Poncho
Hat and Mittens
Joan's Jacket
Shawl

MABLE PONCHO

The warp for this poncho is a sturdy grey commercial wool yarn from J. & H. Clasgens in New Richmond, Ohio. The weft is handspun from the spring 1977 clipping of Mable, one of our grey sheep. The wool was spun in-the-grease and I alternately used darker and lighter parts of the fleece to get a variegated effect.

I don't know just where the inspiration came for the Mable poncho, but *Cut My Cote* by Dorothy K. Burnham certainly helped. I warped up my loom with this simple project in mind — measuring from my neck down my arm to see what width would look good. I decided on a 22½ inch wide warp in a herringbone twill for a subtle texture and pattern effect.

I threaded my loom ten ends per inch. I got the weaving pattern out of *A Handweaver's Pattern Book* by Marguerite P. Davison, page 22, treadling #1. I wove two sections, each 50 inches long, but I would have preferred a longer poncho. I started and ended each section with a few rows of tabby. I hand sewed the front, back, and side seams and finished the bottom edges with warp knotted into fringe. The neck should be reinforced at the seams, as these are points of stress. The finished poncho was then washed since the yarn was spun in-the-grease making the garment stiff and dirty. It's amazing, the difference a little

J. & H. Clasgens Co.
Mill Store
New Richmond, OH 45157

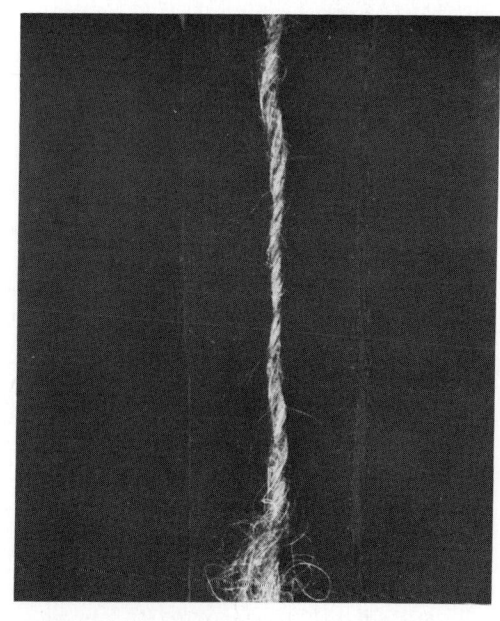

Mable's wool, poncho.

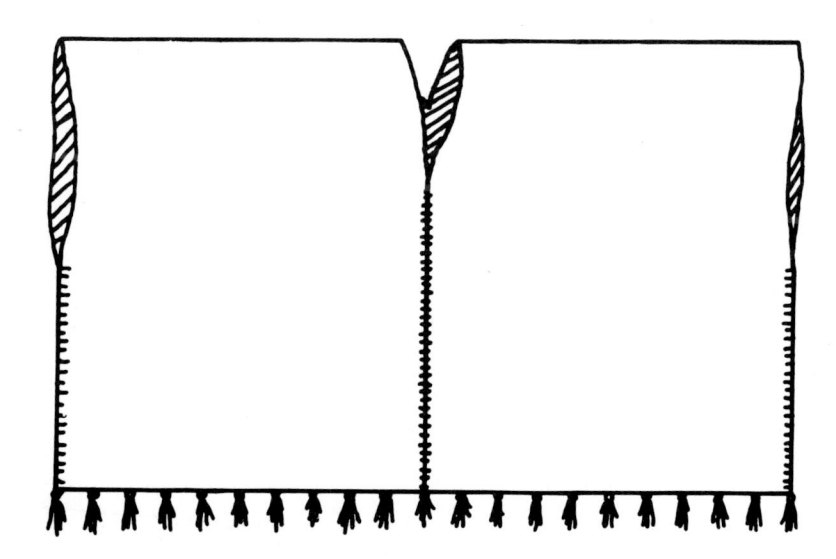

Wool for this poncho supplied by "Mable."
Spun and woven in the grease.

Photograph by Stuart Golder

mild soap and rainwater make on previously unscoured wool. This is a very simple garment to make and can be varied easily by changing length, width, color, weaving pattern, and omitting side seams or fringe. It's easy to make this poncho "your own."

Photograph by Stuart Golder

Detail of poncho, showing warp fringe, striping.

HAT & MITTENS

All the fibers in the hat and mittens are "home grown." The yarn for the mittens was spun from Brillo, who was then a black sheep (he's gotten grey) and Marjorie, a white sheep. For a third color I carded the two together before spinning. The wool was spun thickly on a drop spindle and a treadle sewing machine ganged up as a treadle spindle (obviously a homemade rig). I wrote an article on how to do this; it appears in "Countryside" magazine, December 1977. The two pictures on the second page of the article are mirror images. The hat was crocheted of unspun wool and handspun angora (singles used double) from our rabbits (some grey and some white). To crochet with unspun wool you either pull it out directly from the fleece as if you were going to spin it, or in the case of short or problem fibers, card the wool first and then pull out from the end of the rolag. It might seem that the end product would be very fragile, but it's not. The wool was used right off the sheep and the finished product washed in cold cistern water and mild soap.

The hat was much easier to work on than the mittens because I have several tried and true hat patterns that I'm familiar with. I changed colors every few rows to get a shaded effect in some

Countryside
312 Portland Road
Waterloo, WI 53594

December 1977, Vol. 61, No. 12
pages 42 and 43
"Sewing Machine Turns Into Spinning Wheel"

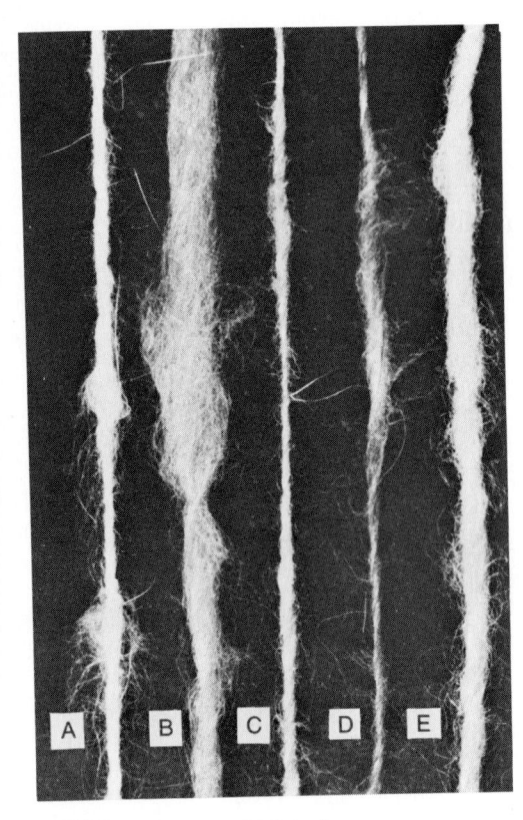

Joan wearing her hat and mittens. Her friend is one of the local sources of fibers.

A White angora rabbit hair.
B Afghan Hound.
C Husky.
D Grey angora.
E Romney.

places and sharp contrast in others. The pattern is one that I found in a magazine about nine years ago and changed a little to suit my needs. I ended up with quite a few oversized hats and a couple of undersized ones before I got a feel for what size yarn, crochet hook, and how tight to work for the desired results.

The directions call for an E hook, but I usually use a G:

Starting at top center, chain (ch) 4. Join with slip stitch (sl st) to form ring.
1st round (rnd): Work 8 single crochet (sc) in ring. Do not join rnds, but mark beginning with a pin.
2nd rnd: Work 2 sc in each sc around (16 sc).
3rd rnd: * Sc in next sc, 2 sc in next sc. Repeat from * around (24 sc).
4th rnd: * Sc in next 2 sc, 2 sc in next sc. Repeat from * around (32 sc).
5th rnd: * Sc in next 3 sc, 2 sc in next sc. Repeat from * around (40 sc).
6th rnd: * Sc in next 4 sc, 2 sc in next sc. Repeat from * around (48 sc).
7th rnd: Sc in each sc around.
8th rnd: * Sc in next 5 sc, 2 sc in next sc. Repeat from * around (56 sc).
9th rnd: Sc in each sc around.
10th rnd: * Sc in next 6 sc, 2 sc in next sc. Repeat from * around (64 sc).
11th rnd: Sc in each sc around.
12th rnd: * Sc in next 7 sc, 2 sc in next sc. Repeat from * around (72 sc).
13th rnd: Sc in each sc around. Repeat last rnd until piece reaches desired length. If you make a hat without a cuff you may want to run elastic through the last round to help the hat keep its shape.

I'd been making handspun hats to sell for a couple of years before I tackled my first pair of mittens. I couldn't find a "pattern" for any that I liked, so I started out the way I would for a single crochet hat — spiraling out from the center. I tried the mitten on after every round and made the necessary adjustments. I worked the top part of the hand and the thumb in this way, attached the two together, and then continued on around the whole thing, decreasing to the wrist and continuing even for the cuff. It's much easier to make a mitten if you have the proper-sized hand around to try on every round or so, but if you can't keep a hand nearby a tracing will do.

For the mittens have two balls of yarn (a small one for the thumb) and try starting out the same as the hat, then skip from directions for the first round to directions for the third round, then the fourth round. If the mitten looks like it will fit over your four fingers, continue even until it hits the base of your thumb. If it doesn't fit, increase a few more stitches in the next row, or rip out a row and don't increase as much, then continue even. Set this part aside (don't break off the yarn) and work the thumb in a similar manner until it's the proper length. End off the thumb leaving a ten-inch piece of yarn which is used to sew the thumb onto the first part of the mitten. Just sew through two or three stitches, then pick up where you left off on the mitten and crochet all around the two parts, gradually decreasing down to the cuff, then continuing even for the desired length. The mittens will fit either hand. Don't get discouraged if it takes a couple of tries before you have good control over the size and fit.

The hat and mittens are simple to make and not too time consuming. So many variations can be made with color and texture. Turn the items inside out for a different look or brush them with a stiff brush to raise the nap and give a fuzzy effect.

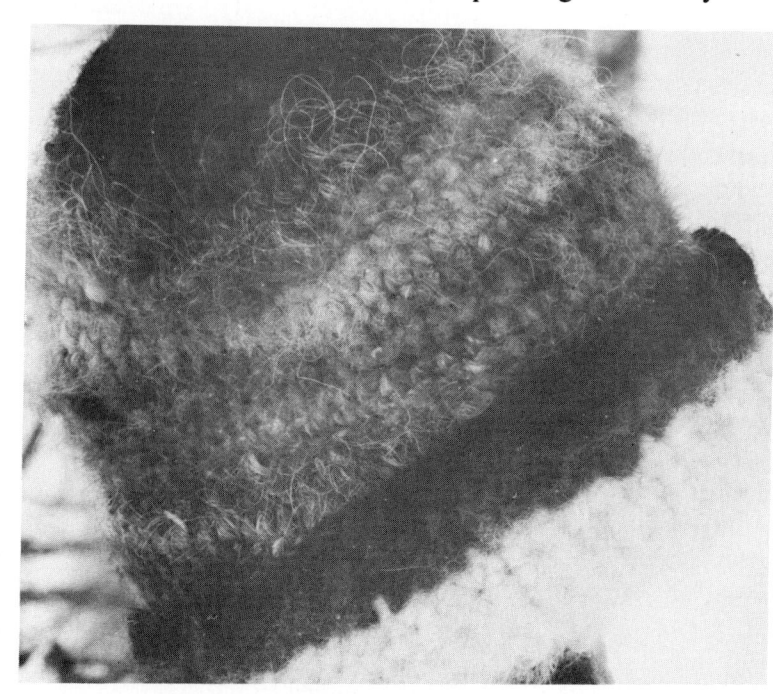

Photograph by Stuart Golder

Detail of hat. Crocheted from unspun wool and handspun angora rabbit hair.

JOAN'S JACKET

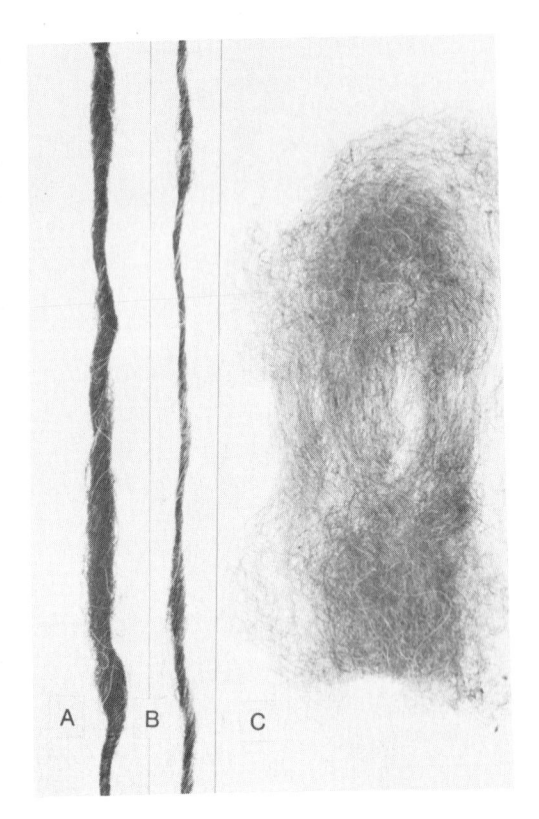

When I taught myself to spin in 1973, the first thing I wanted to make myself was a jacket. It took me four years to get around to it since I had to teach myself to weave, buy a place in the country, raise sheep and angora rabbits, and scrape together the money for a loom before I could get started.

The warp is a sturdy grey wool yarn from Clasgens Woolen Mill in New Richmond, Ohio. The weft is handspun from our sheep and angora rabbits and friends' dogs. The fibers were all spun unwashed and in their natural colors. The lining material is a cotton blend from Hancock's Fabric Store in Cincinnati, Ohio. I like the contrast of the red lining and the subdued tones of the jacket, but many people don't.

The idea for the jacket came from a workshop on loom-shaped clothing sponsored by the Weavers' Guild of Greater Cincinnati. It was given by Roz Berlin. This was my first "formal" instruction in weaving. Everything had to be completely thought out before warping the loom — lots of measurements taken and consideration given to shrinkage, etc. I decided against slits on the sides at the lower hem, but after wearing the jacket, feel they would have been a good idea because of the way I'm built. I put in gussets to give me freedom of movement without widening the body or sleeves. I added a hood and pockets because I like hoods — they keep my neck and head warm, and I like pockets — a good place to keep my hands and other things.

I used a ten dent reed, double sleyed for double weave — a tubular tabby. The warp should have an uneven number of threads so there aren't two together at one edge. If, when weaving, one layer falls behind the other, throw in a few extra shots on the lagging edge. The inside of the tube will probably have a better look than the outside along the folds. A good way to check the bottom layer for mistakes while weaving is with a mirror. Check often. A horizontal seam can be woven in with a shot of tabby, both layers together. Any place I intended to have a seam allowance or hem I wove in thinner yarn for less bulk. Weave tissue or rags in places where nothing is to be woven to keep the tension even. I tried to make the bottom half of my sleeves darker so they wouldn't show up dirt as quickly as light colors.

Measure carefully for the jacket, allow for shrinkage when removing from the loom and when washing. The measurements given are what I used for myself and won't fit everybody. When figuring the hood length, measure from the center top of the head to the shoulder and allow a little extra. For hood width, measure from the forehead to the top back "corner" of the head (for example, if it's about 10", then weave 5" of hood on each side of front center slit and 10" across the back). When measuring for sleeves, figure width of widest part of arm (shoulder to armpit?), length from armpit to wrist, and from

A Young 1/2 breed karakul (Brillo).
B 1/2 breed karakul, older (Brillo).
C Unspun karakul (Hershey, Brillo's father).

Detail of jacket

Also shown in color.

Photograph by Stuart Golder

Photograph by Stuart Golder

Joan's jacket. Wool, angora rabbit hair, dog hair.

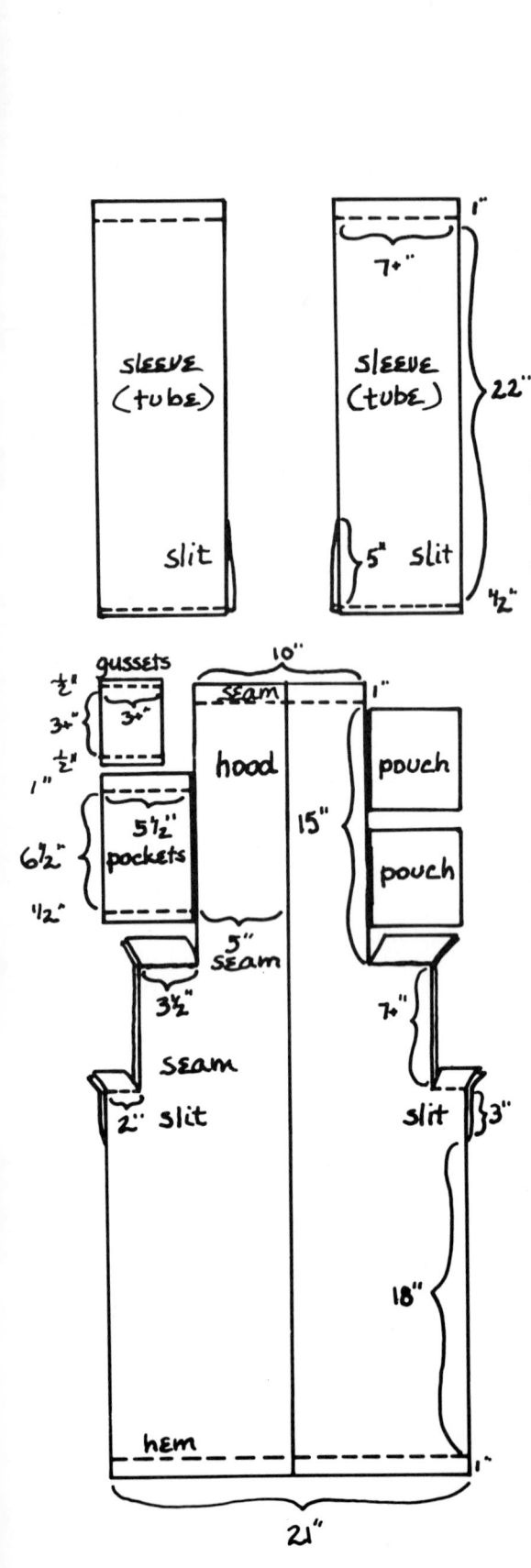

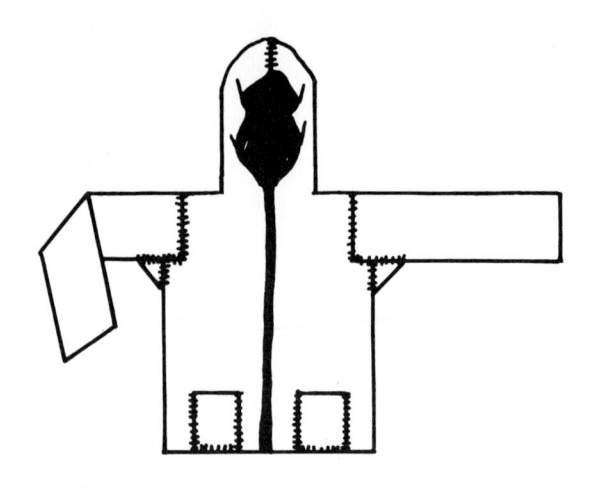

shoulder to wrist. Shoulders should be measured from neck edge to shoulder edge. Remember, if the loom is warped for a 21" width the finished product will be 42" around, less shrinkage.

The gussets and sleeves were sewn on with Afghan Hound hair. Fold the gussets diagonally and sew half to front body and sleeve, half to back. The hood seam gets folded and sewn from front to back, not side to side like it was woven. The jacket and lining were washed separately, then sewn together by hand and machine. My husband, Stuart Golder, made the buttons of prunings from our apple trees and button loops were made of leather lacing.

Feel free to experiment. A much simpler jacket can be woven with dropped shoulder seams, wider sleeves, and no gussets. Instead of weaving 15" for a hood, weave 5" and have a collar. The lining can be left out and fringes left on. Wrap it and belt it instead of putting on buttons and loops. Above all, have fun with it!

SHAWL

The fibers for this shawl are handspun natural white "top" from Clasgens Woolen Mill, New Richmond, Ohio, and a very lightweight pink and blue variegated yarn which I bought on sale at Clasgens because it was cheap and I thought it would be fun to experiment with even though I didn't like the colors. I'd used lightweight yarn as warp before and had problems with it breaking so I was much more careful this time and put a lot less tension on the warp. I used a 12 dent reed and threaded my loom about two feet wide in a Swedish lace weave: Lace Stripe, page 96 in *A Handweaver's Pattern Book* by Marguerite Porter Davison. I wanted to take advantage of the lightweight yarn and produce an airy summer shawl. I also was curious to see what would happen with the variegated yarn when it was used as just warp, and as both warp and weft. The result in the latter case was a mottled purple color that people found very attractive.

When spinning the "top" I wanted to get a fairly thin and even yarn. I'd break off a yard or so of top, then split it into thirds to make it easier to spin. I used the warp for three shawls. The other two have homegrown and handspun angora in them. Each shawl is about five or six feet long. I prefer longer shawls. Remember to take shrinkage into account when figuring size. The shawl is finished off with simple knotted fringe.

Photograph by Stuart Golder

Also shown in color.   Detail of shawl. Handspun weft, fine singles spun from top.

Suppliers' Directory

The Black Sheep
1010 First Street
The Old Market
Encinitas, California 92024
(See page 44)

J. & H. Clasgens Co.
Mill Store
New Richmond, Ohio 45157
(Wool source, see page 73)

Clemes & Clemes Spinning Wheels
650 San Pablo Avenue
Pinole, California 94564
(Fiber source, see page 31)

W. Cushing & Company
Kennebunkport, Maine 04046
(Dye source, see page 3)

Custom Handweavers
Allied Arts Guild
Arbor Road and Creek Drive
Menlo Park, California 94025
(Mohair source, see page 59)

Rita Dayton
Box 887
Simi Valley, California 93065
(Wool source, see page 57)

Earth Guild/Grateful Union
Mail Order Service
Hot Springs, North Carolina 28743
(Dye source, see page 62)

Greentree Ranch Wools
163 N. Carter Lake Road
Loveland, Colorado 80537
(Wool source, see page 22)

Haber/Zemel/Tryon Wool
325 Harbor Way
South San Francisco, California 94080
(Wool source, see pages 61, 62)

Hedgehog Equipment
Forest Craft Center
Upper Hartfield, East Sussex, England
(Wool source, see page 1)

The Mannings
R.D.2
East Berlin, Pennsylvania 17316
(Dye source, see page 60)

Mountain Weaver
P.O. Box 1734
334 N. Santa Cruz
Los Gatos, California 95030
(Wool source, see page 59)

Rose Garden of the Ozarks
Route 2, Box 121A
Willow Springs, Missouri 65793
(See page 58)

Santa Cruz Weaver's Supply
1001 Center Street
P.O. Box 1294
Santa Cruz, California 95061
(Wool source, see pages 61, 62)

Scott's Woolen Mill
Hecla Street and Elmdale Road
Uxbridge, Massachusetts 01569
(Wool source, page 69)

Straw Into Gold
5533 College Avenue
Oakland, California 94618
(Dye source, see page 62)

Studio of Handcrafts
P.O. Box 686
5405 Aura Avenue
Tarzana, California 91356
(Cashmere source, see page 53)

The Wool Factory
1246 N. Hwy. 101
Leucadia, California 92024
(Wool source, see page 44)

Photographers

Karl Runkle	*807 West Clark* *Champaign, Illinois 61820*
Grenier-Ducharme	*Baystate West* *Mall Level* *Springfield, Massachusetts 01103*
Douglas Nidiffer	*P.O. Box 1* *Brookings, Oregon 97415*
Cougar Photography	*104 Main Street* *Montpelier, Vermont 05602*
Creative Photography	*T. Fred* *409 Cameron Circle #501* *Chattanooga, Tennessee 37403*
Les Rodrigues	*259 26th Street* *Del Mar, California 92014*
McBride Photography	*14944 Sherman Way, B204* *Van Nuys, California 91405*
Mary Ellen Schultz	*1060 Furlong Street* *Belmont, California 94002*
Sandra Wallin	*Wallin Forge* *Rt. 1, Box 65* *Sparta, Kentucky 41086*

Bibliography

Burnham, Dorothy K.	*Cut My Cote.*
Davenport, Elsie G.	*Your Handspinning.* Select Books 1964
Davison, Marguerite P.	*A Handweaver's Pattern Book.* Marguerite P. Davison, Publisher
Dawson, Mary M.	*A Complete Guide to Crochet Stitches.* Crown 1973
Grae, Ida	*Nature's Colors: Dyes from Plants.* Macmillan 1974
MacKenzie, Clinton	*New Design in Crochet.* Van Nostrand Reinhold 1972
Naumann, Rose & Hull, Raymond	*The Off-Loom Weaving Book.* Charles Scribner's Sons 1973
Simmons, Paula	*Spinning and Weaving with Wool.* Pacific Search Press 1977
Sommers, Elyse and Mike	*A New Look at Knitting.* Crown 1977
Thomas, Mary	*Mary Thomas's Knitting Book.* Dover 1972
Wilson, Jean	*Pile Weaves.* Van Nostrand Reinhold; 1974 *Weaving You Can Wear.* Van Nostrand Reinhold 1973
Zimmerman, Elizabeth	*Knitter's Almanac.* Charles Scribner's Sons 1974

Index

A

Acorns 62
Afghan 41, 42
Afghan hound hair 80
Alpaca 36, 68
    Peruvian 43
    roving 69
Alum 8, 11, 22, 24, 25, 26, 30
Ammonia 24, 25, 26
Angora
    goats 24, 35
    handspun 81
    rabbits 75, 78
Antique spinning wheels 1, 51
Apple leaves 11
Ashford spinning wheel 12, 31, 35, 65, 66, 71
Asian camel down 43

B

Baby blanket 29, 30, 34
Bag
    bound weave 14
    handspun karakul 49, 50
    tapestry 31
    tote 56, 57
Basket weave 35
Baskets, crochet 47, 48, 61-63
Bedspread
    overshot weave 11-13
    handspun warp 13, 14
    handspun warp and weft 68-72
Berlin, Roz 78
Birch leaves 11
Blanket 68-72
Blocking
    knitted shawl 32
Border, decorative 21
Bound weave 14
Braid 44
Broom sedge 8
Bulky yarn 3, 6, 7, 24, 35, 49
Buttons
    apple wood 80
    antler 67
    bone 67
    crochet 23
    pottery 67

C

Calculations, weaving 8
Camel hair 42
    Asian camel down 43
    baby camel 52
    Mongolian baby 53
Camels 53
Carrot tops 48
Cashmere 52, 56
Castle wheel 67
Cheviot Cross 51
Cheviot wool 18
Cholla cactus 59
Chrome 8, 11, 13, 24, 25, 26, 30, 31
Coat, handwoven 51, 52
Cochineal 13
Collie dog hair 14, 17
Columbian sheep 31, 51
Commercial dyes 3
Commercial yarn
    see yarn, commercial
Coreopsis 11
Copper sulphate 13
Coralline 59
Corriedale 61
Cost, of blanket 68
Cotton, commercial warp 11, 14, 17, 56
Cream of tartar 13, 22
Crochet
    baskets 47, 48, 61, 62
    decorative banding 8
    dog hair 2
    hat 75
    mittens 77
    on hoop 60
    ornamentation 7, 48
    over a core 48
    pillows 2
    shawl 4
    unspun fleece 75
    vest 21-23
    wall hanging 6
    weed bag 5

D

Dahlia flower heads (lavender) 22
Desert pinion 42
Direct dye-bath 62
Direct tie-up 14
Dog hair 2, 78
    Afghan hound 80
    collie 14, 17
    combining with wool 2, 3
    crochet 2
    English sheepdog 2
    Huskie-shepherd 2, 3
    Newfoundland 18
Dorset 65, 67
Double drive band 44
Double-faced fabric 52
Drop spindle 10, 18
Dye pot 36, 59
Dyestuffs
    acorns 62
    apple leaves 11
    birch leaves 11
    broom sedge 8
    carrot tops 48
    cochineal 13
    commercial 3
    coralline 59
    coreopsis 11
    dahlia flower heads 22
    desert pinion 42
    eucalyptus leaves 14
    forget-me-not (roots) 42
    foxglove flowers 22
    goldenrod 24, 25, 30, 31
    horsetails 24, 26
    lily of the valley leaves 10, 11
    marigolds 13, 24
    marsh marigolds 24
    mullein 24
    onion skins 8, 24, 30, 42, 61
    sagebush 24, 30
    St. Johnswort 24
    wood, exotic 62
Dyeing
    contact 24, 36, 59, 62
    handspun bulky yarns 3
    naturally 8, 10, 11, 13, 14, 22, 24, 25, 31, 35
    space 3
    unspun fleece 3, 11

E

Eggs, wire 61
Embroidery 8
English sheepdog hair 2
Eucalyptus leaves (dollar) 14
Ewes 65
   fleece 66, 67

F

Felting 38
Finnish castle wheel 67
Flax, handspun 12
Flax wheel 1, 31
Fleece
   Columbian 51
   Corriedale 61
   Dorset 65, 67
   ewes 66, 67
   inlay technique with 36
   Gobelins 10
   karakul 36, 38, 61
   Merino 8
   Romney 11
      New Zealand 17, 44, 69
   Speilslau 69
   Suffolk 22, 35, 67
   using up extra 36
   washing 12, 22, 24, 31, 49, 62, 69
   Western 67
Floating selvedge thread 14
Forget-me-not (roots) 42
Foxglove flowers (purple) 22
Fringe
   knotted 5, 6, 7, 38, 81
   pillows 2
   tied 3
   warp 14, 25, 72, 73
   woven 12

G

Gauge 5, 19, 21, 28, 31, 32, 53, 58
Gloves 18-20
Goldenrod 24, 25, 30, 31
Great wheel 65
Gussets 78

H

Handles, interchangeable 57
Handspinning
   bulky weight yarn 2
   in the grease 8, 24, 31, 44, 58, 69, 73
   on a Navajo spindle 1
   problems, overspin 1
   short draw 53
   uncarded wool 41
   warp yarns 42, 65
Handspun yarn
   see yarn, handspun
Handweavers and Craftsman Magazine 17
Hangings, wall
   see wall hangings
Hat
   knitted 28, 57, 58, 66, 67
   crochet 75-77
Hood 44, 47, 78
Horsetails 24, 26
Huskie-shepherd hair 2, 3

I

Inlay 36, 49
Iron 24, 30, 62

J

Jacket
   knitted, man's 65, 66
   woven
      hooded 44, 45, 47
      Joan's 78-80
      kimono 8-10
Johansen spinning wheel 44
Jumbo spinner head 2, 6
Jute 61

K

Karakul 36, 38, 42, 49, 50, 61
Kashmir 52
Kashmir goats 53
Killim slits 17
Kircher spinning wheel 24
Knitting
   baby blanket 29, 30, 34
   cardigan
      child's 28, 66
      girl's 67
   circles 32
   circular shawl 31, 32, 33
   gloves 19
   hats 57
   jacket, man's 65
   scarves 52
   squares 32
   sweater, woman's 26-28
   vest 58
Knotted fringe 5, 6, 7, 38, 81

L

Lark head knotting 38
Lichen, rock 11
Lily of the valley leaves 10, 11
Linen 10
Llama 36
Loom
   four-harness 3, 44
   home constructed 10
   jack, 4-harness 12
   Pendleton 35, 42
   Structo, 4-harness, table 42
Loom shaped 78

M

Marigolds 13, 24, 26
Marsh Marigolds 24, 26
Merino 8
mittens 75, 77
Mohair 25, 29, 31, 36, 38, 43, 61, 68, 69
Mongolian baby camel hair 52, 53
Mordant
   alum 8, 11, 13, 24, 25, 26, 30, 59
   ammonia 24, 25, 26
   chrome 8, 11, 13, 24, 25, 26, 30, 31, 59
   copper 59
   iron 24, 30, 59, 62
   tin 59
Mounting rod 7
Mullein 24, 25

N

Natural dyes
   see dyestuffs
Navajo spindle 1, 3
Newfoundland dog hair 18
New Zealand
   Romney 17, 41, 42, 44
   wool 36, 43, 57, 59

O

Off-loom weaving 59
Oil, spinning 69
Onion skins 8, 24, 30, 42, 61
Overshot weave 11, 14
Overspin 1, 12

P

Panama sheep 31
Paragon wheel 59, 62
Pattern
   books 5
   commercial 58
   clothing 51
   gauge 5, 21
   glove 19, 20
   hat 57, 75, 76
   knitting 65
   repeat 58
   weaving 11

Penguin quill wheel 47
Pillows 2, 3
Plying yarn 18, 69, 71
Pockets 78
Poncho, woven 25, 26, 42, 43, 73-75

Q

Quantities
    dog hair 2
    fleece 12
    yarn 5, 9, 10, 14, 23, 25, 31, 32, 34, 52, 72

Quesquemtle 25

R

Rambouillet 56, 57
Rod, mounting 7
Romney
    New Zealand 17, 41, 42, 44
    sheep 24, 28
    wool 11, 22, 28, 69
Roving 47, 48, 58
    mohair 61
Rugs
    inlay raw fleece 36-38
    Swedish rosepath 42
Runner, rainbow 35, 36

S

Sagebush 24, 30
St. Johnswort 24, 26
Salish
    blankets 11
    frame 10
    Indians 11
Sample swatches
    crochet 5, 21
    knitted 27, 58, 66
    woven 8
Saxony wheel 44, 65
Scarves, cashmere 52-54, 56
Sett 8, 42, 44
Sewing
    hand
        bag, handles 50
        baby blanket 34
        fringe 12
        jacket 80
            braid 44
            kimono 8
        poncho 25, 73
        sweater 28
        vest
            crochet 23
            knitted 59
    machine
        bag, zipper 50
        jacket 47
Shawl
    crochet 4
    knit, circular 31-34
    woven 80, 81
Shoulder strap, bag 14
Shrinkage 43, 50, 78, 81
Simmons, Paula 1
Slits 78
Speilslau 69
Spindles
    drop 10, 18
    Navajo 1, 3
Spinning oil 69
Spinning wheels
    antique 1, 51
    Ashford 8, 12, 31, 65, 66, 71
    castle 67
    Finnish castle 67
    flax 1
    great 65
    Johansen 44
    Kircher 24
    Paragon 59, 62
    Penguin quill 47
    saxony 44, 65
    Toika Flyer 49
    treadle sewing machine 1, 75
    walking 65
Stannous chloride 13
stole, crocheted 4, 5
stole, woven 3, 4
stretcher (temple) 14
Stripes, use in
    bedspread 13
    gloves 18, 19
    hat 57, 75
    jacket 44
    kimono jacket 8
    knitting 18, 19, 53, 57
    rainbow runner 36
    scarves 53
    tote bag 56
    warp 13, 44
    weft 8, 36, 56
Suffolk 22, 35, 67
Sweater
    cardigan
        child's 28, 66
    girl's 67
    man's 65, 66
    pullover 26-28
Swedish lace weave 80

T

Tabby weave 3, 36, 44, 49, 56
    weft 52
Tapestry 10
Tapestry weave 17
Targee (crossbred) 31
Temple (stretcher) 14
Textural interest 7
Toika Flyer wheel 49
Treadle sewing machine spinning wheel 75
Twig bags 5
Tubular weave 78
Twill weave 14
    herringbone 73
    three-and-one 52, 72
Twining 10

V

Variegated yarn 73
Velcro 14
Vest
    crochet 21-23
    knitted 58, 59

W

Walking wheel 65
Wall hangings
    crochet 6, 7
    woven 10, 11, 16, 17, 36-38, 59-61
Warp-faced 72
Warp yardage 10
Warping reel 13
Washing
    bedspread 13, 14
    cashmere 56
    finished work 30, 38, 50, 58, 73, 75
    fleece 12, 22, 24, 31, 49, 62, 69
    sheep 31
    yarn 12, 18, 22, 24, 44, 49, 58, 71
Weaving
    afghan 41
    bag 14, 31, 49, 56
    bedspread 11, 12, 13
    blanket 68-72
    calculations 8, 9
    coat 51, 52
    fleece 36
    fringe 12
    in the grease 36, 73
    hanging 10, 17, 36
    jacket 8, 44, 78
    poncho 25, 42, 73
    rug 36, 42
    runner 35
    shawl 80

stole 3
unspun fleece 36

Weed bag 5, 6

Weft-faced 71, 72

Wire eggs 61

Western (sheep) 67

Wood, exotic 62

Wool

Cheviot 18
Cheviot Cross 51
Columbian (Sheep) 31, 51
commercially dyed 58
Corriedale 61
Dorset 65, 67
Gobelins 10
karakul 36, 38, 42, 49, 50, 61
Merino 8
New Zealand 36, 57, 59
  Romney 17, 41, 42, 44
Panama (sheep) 31
Rambouillet 56, 57
Romney 11, 69
roving 47, 48, 58
Speilslau 69
Suffolk 22, 35, 67
Targee 31
top 80
Western (sheep) 67

Y

Yarn, commercial

alpaca 43
  -llama mix 44
Bartlettsyarn wool singles 52
Bartlettsyarn wool warp 52
boucle wool 3
carpet warp 14, 17
cotton warp 11, 56
"Cum" warp 42
"Curlama" (Berroco) 61
Greek goat hair 47
heavy 61
jute, 3 ply 61
knitting worsted 6
medium weight wool 25
mohair (handspun) 59
novelty 56
rug 59
  wool 36, 50
synthetic-wool blend 3
substituting handspun for 5
tweed 14
variegated 80
warp
  carpet 14, 17
  cotton 11, 56
  "Cum" 42
  rug 35
wool
  boucle 3
  medium weight 25

nylon, angora blend 8
rug 36, 50
rug warp 35
sturdy 73, 78
Woolspinneri Alpen Wool

Yarn, handspun

beginner's 4, 65
bulky 3, 6, 7, 24, 35, 49
coarse, slubby 10
controlled slub 56
double spun, warp 31
fine, uniform 67
hairy, tweedy 49
loose twist 58
lumpy 26
medium fine, 2 ply 66
medium weight, single ply 3
mohair, naturally dyed 29
plyed 12, 18, 42, 69
  with novelty yarn 56
rough textured 62
slub, controlled 56
smooth, medium twist 17
thick and thin 22, 24, 59
thin
  even 81
  single-ply 53
underspun 66
uneven 24
variegated 73
warp 69
  double spun 31